NEW CLAIT

SUE PRICE

In easy steps is an imprint of Computer Step
Southfield Road . Southam
Warwickshire CV47 0FB . United Kingdom
www.ineasysteps.com

Endorsed by OCR for use with the OCR Level 1 Certificate
for IT Users (New CLAIT)

Notice of Liability

Trademarks

Printed and bound in the United Kingdom

ISBN 1-84078-209-9

Contents

Graphs and charts 147

7

Computer art 167

8

Using a computer

This unit is mandatory if you wish to achieve the New CLAIT certificate. The unit covers the basics of starting a computer, using a password, accessing a file and adding text, saving files and printing.

Covers

Unit One

Your computer

Your computer may look like the one illustrated, with many separate pieces of hardware, or it may be as compact as a laptop, but it should fundamentally consist of the same elements.

The systems unit

This is where the disk drives, memory chips and adapter cards are located. The main hard disk is the storage area for programs that are loaded onto your computer. Its size or capacity for storage is measured in gigabytes (approximately one thousand million bytes). The unit also contains the floppy drive, the CD drive and maybe a DVD drive.

The disk drives on your computer are referred to by a letter followed by a colon. The hard disk inside the systems unit is usually known as the C: drive, and the floppy disk as the A: drive.

The memory is where the activity takes place on the computer. When you create or change a document the information is held in memory until you save it to disk. The memory chips are measured in megabytes (approximately one million bytes).

The adapter cards allow you to attach hardware, such as a monitor, keyboard, mouse and printer.

A resolution of 800 by 600 will give you larger text and icons on your monitor, but the detail will not be as fine.

The monitor

The monitor has two measurements - the actual physical size which is expressed in inches or centimetres, and the resolution which is measured in pixels (picture elements). Most monitors use a resolution of 1024 by 768. The number of colours you can use is 256, 64 thousand (16 bit) or 16 million (32 bit).

The function key, F1, takes you to Help in most programs.

In computing, a space is treated as a character. Use the right arrow, not the spacebar, to move the cursor to the right.

The arrow keys, Home, End, Page Up and Page Down allow you to move around your document.

Single click the mouse to select an item, double click the item to apply an action such as Open.

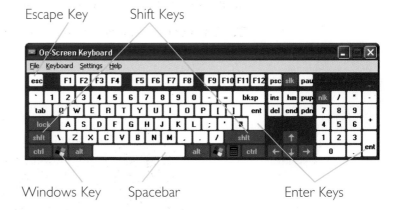

If you are left-handed you can exchange the actions. Select Start, Settings, Control Panel, Mouse.

The keyboard

There are many different styles of keyboard – standard, ergonomically designed, ones with built-in wrist rests and even some with programmable keys. It is worth studying the keyboard before you switch the computer on.

The standard keyboard has 105 keys. You will see the normal qwerty keys in the central section with number keys above. Below the letters is the spacebar. To the left and right of the letters are the shift keys, indicated by an arrow on each pointing forwards. You must press and hold the shift key to get the symbols on the number keys. Also press the shift key to get a single capital letter. The Caps Lock key is for a series of capitals. The large key to the right of the letters is the Enter or Carriage Return key.

Escape Key   Shift Keys

Windows Key   Spacebar   Enter Keys

On the right is the number keypad, with its own set of mathematical symbols (+-*/) and Enter key. To get numbers the Num Lock light must be on.

The mouse

There are mice with two buttons, three buttons or scrolling wheels. The first or left mouse button is used as Enter or to select an item. Mouse button two or the right button presents different menus depending on which item is selected. The function of the third or centre button also varies. If you have a three button mouse check the manual to see what other functions are available – you may need to install additional software to enable them.

The software

The operating system

The most important piece of software on your computer is the operating system. This is the program that allows you to use the keyboard, disk drives, monitor etc. It also allows you to use other programs such as the word processor.

There are several operating systems including Windows, Apple Mac and Unix. In this book we are using Windows XP. If your operating system software is a different version of Windows (other than Windows 3.x), you will still be able to use this book, as there are few differences between the versions at the New CLAIT level of use.

Microsoft Office XP

In this book we are using the Office XP Professional package which provides the full range of software required to complete all the New CLAIT units.

Microsoft sells Office XP in versions which do not have all the programs – you may find, for example, that Access in not included in your copy of Office XP.

The following list identifies each CLAIT unit with the appropriate Office XP program:

You should be able to follow the illustrations and guides, even if you have a different release of Office, as the methods to complete the activities required by New CLAIT are almost identical in all releases.

- Unit 1   Using a computer   Windows

- Unit 2   Word Processing   Word

- Unit 3   Electronic Communication   Outlook Express Internet Explorer

- Unit 4   Spreadsheets   Excel

- Unit 5   Databases   Access

- Unit 6   Desktop Publishing   Publisher

- Unit 7   Graphs and Charts   Excel

- Unit 8   Computer Art   Word

- Unit 9   Web Pages   FrontPage

- Unit 10   Presentation Graphics   PowerPoint

Your workstation

Your computer and its surrounding equipment, such as printer, desk, chair and telephone is known as your workstation. You should design the layout of your workstation so that you sit correctly and can reach most of the equipment easily, without undue strain or stretching.

Repetitive Strain Injury (RSI) can be caused by sitting incorrectly at your computer.

1   The correct sitting position is with your thighs parallel to the floor and your feet flat on the floor or on a foot rest. If you cannot adjust your chair, use a cushion. Your back should be straight and well supported. Your arms should be relaxed and hang straight from the shoulder, with your forearms parallel to the floor and your wrists straight, not bent awkwardly.

2   The keyboard should be adjustable and at a comfortable height. The mouse should be near the keyboard and easy to reach.

Document or copy stands are very useful. They should be positioned close to the monitor and at the same height.

3   The monitor should be at the proper viewing distance, between 18 and 24 inches away, directly in front of you rather than at an angle. The height should be adjusted so that you can look slightly down at it. It should also be at right angles to the window or light source to avoid glare.

4   You should take short breaks to prevent muscle fatigue, get up once in a while and walk around. Look away from the monitor from time to time to relax your eyes.

Starting the computer

You will need to switch on the systems unit and possibly the monitor. Some monitors are powered through the systems unit, and some are independently powered. It is worth turning on the monitor first, as you will be able to read any information and error messages as the computer starts up.

As the computer starts, it goes through a process called the Power On Self Test (POST). It will check its memory and the hardware attached – you may see the keyboard lights flash, and hear the printer reset. Make sure that there is no floppy data disk in the drive when you start up, since this will interfere with the start up process. If you do leave a disk in the drive by mistake, just follow the instructions to remove the disk and press any key to continue.

The password

The New CLAIT course requires that you are able to use a password to logon and access a data file. The logon and password may be required as the computer starts, as illustrated here, or it may be required to access a particular file. For security reasons, when you type in your password it will be disguised as a series of asterisks or dots. The question mark allows you to view a password hint. You can create a password hint when you set the password.

It is also possible to set passwords on individual files. In Word, select Tools, Options and the Security tab. Specify a password and click OK.

The hourglass symbol lets you know that the computer is busy.

Once the ID and password have been accepted, the operating system will continue to load. The Windows desktop screen will appear with a series of pictures or icons on the left side of the monitor. You must wait until the hourglass symbol disappears and becomes an arrow before you can begin to work.

Once the operating system is fully loaded, you will see the desktop. The standard desktop has icons (graphical representations) down the left side of the screen. At the bottom is the Taskbar, with the Start button, Quick Launch bar, and to the right is the System tray.

The Icons

My Computer gives you a view of the hardware and software that is installed on your PC.

My Documents takes you to the folder where all your data files are stored.

Recycle Bin is where you put files you wish to delete.

To see total capacity, used space and free space on your C: drive, double click My Computer, then single click the C: drive. Click with the right mouse button on the drive icon and from the menu, select Properties.

My Documents

My Computer

Shortcut to Word

Recycle Bin

Shortcut to Floppy drive

Active window with contents of a folder

The Taskbar

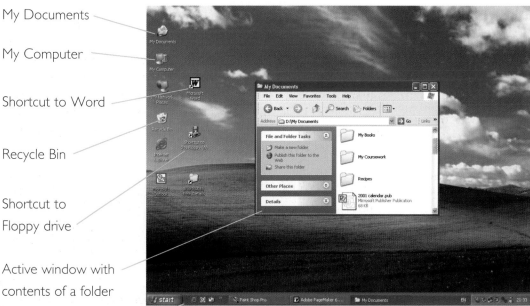

Internet Explorer can be used as the Internet browser, although you may decide to use an alternative.

There are other standard icons, for example My Network Places. Icons may appear when you install new hardware or software and you can create shortcut icons for yourself which will take you directly to an application, data file or hardware item.

The Start menu and Taskbar

The Start Menu

Click the Start button with the left mouse button. This is the standard way to start using the computer. It gives you access to programs, documents and utilities such as searching for a file.

Any programs that you use frequently will be listed above the Start button. For other programs, move the mouse to All programs, wait a moment and the next level of menu will appear. Move the mouse across and up to the application you want. Then click again.

Selecting My Documents from the Start menu opens the My Documents folder. You can then double click on an existing file to open it.

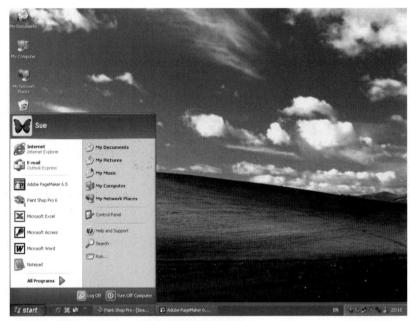

You may find that the Taskbar is positioned at the top or side of the screen. Click and hold the mouse arrow on a clear section. You can then drag and drop it to which ever edge you prefer.

The Taskbar

The Quick Launch bar opens the application selected. Hover the mouse over the icons to view the purpose of each.

Any applications which are currently running will show on the Taskbar. The active application or window will appear indented (see page 13). As the Taskbar fills, the buttons shrink. Click the program name to see a list of files open in that application.

Hover the mouse over the time to see the date.

The System Tray on the right of the Taskbar shows the time, and utilities such as the virus checker and dialup connection status.

A standard window

The same basic elements comprise a window, whether it is a folder window, or a program window.

If you cannot see the toolbar, select View, Toolbars, Standard Buttons.

These buttons allow you to expand and contract the frame to see more options.

File and Folder Tasks

Title bar   Menu bar   Minimise   Maximise/Restore

Close

Toolbar

Scroll bar

Status bar   selected item   Resize position

To move a window, click and drag the Title bar.

The bright blue Title bar indicates that it is the active window. If the Title bar is pale blue, click in the window to reactivate it.

The Menu bar contains the full list of options for this window.

The blue pane on the left provides access to file and folder tasks, such as copying and deleting files. It also provides details on the selected item, as does the Status bar if visible.

The Toolbar allows you to navigate the folders. Some of the buttons have tips, revealed if you hover the mouse over them.

The Scroll bars only appear when there is too much information to fit the size of the window. Click the arrows at each end of the scroll bar, or hold and drag the sliding bar.

The minimise button shrinks the window but leaves it available on the Taskbar. The Maximise/Restore button toggles between full screen and window. The Close button closes the current window. If it is an application window, the program will check if you wish to save any previously unsaved data.

Exploring files and folders

Your hard disk, the C: drive is like a very large filing cabinet. Files that you create (data files), and the files that the computer uses (system files), are stored in folders on the hard disk. To see an overview of the structure of the filing system:

It is possible to move (drag and drop) folders in Explorer inadvertently, so be careful with the mouse.

1 Click Start, All Programs, Accessories, Windows Explorer.

2 The Explorer window is divided into two panes. The left pane gives the structure of the folder organisation. The right pane shows the files and folders within the selected folder, in this case My Documents.

Select View, List, from the Menu bar to increase the number of files visible at once. Select View, Details, to see file size, date etc.

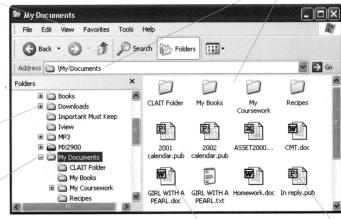

Click the + symbol next to a yellow folder in the left pane to expand the subfolder list. Click the [-] symbol to contract it.

3 The file icons indicate the file type - W for Word, P for Publisher, X for Excel etc. You can double click a folder in the right pane to open it and view the contents. If you double click a file it will open in the associated application.

When you are working on this course, it is a good idea to create your own work folder. This will help you to keep all the files together, making it easier to manage them. It is also good working practice, whether in an office or home situation.

You may create your folder on the A: drive or on the hard disk. When you have created your own folder, open Windows Explorer, (see page 16) and check that it is in the desired location.

4 Office applications save data files into the My Documents folder, so you could create your work folder here.

5 Double click the My Documents folder on the desktop to open it. Make sure that you have no files or folders selected.

If you have a file or folder selected, the New entry on the File menu is further down in the list.

6 Select File, New, Folder. Type the name of the folder and press Enter.

7 Double click on the folder to open it, or single click and press Enter.

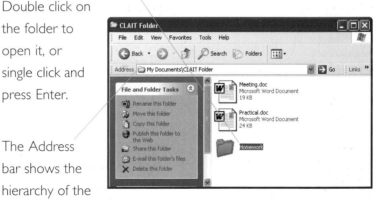

To rename the folder, select the folder, right click and select Rename from the menu. Type the new name and press Enter.

8 The Address bar shows the hierarchy of the folders.

9 When you use the Open or Save file function in an application, you will see the new folder listed.

Using Search to find files

One of your first New CLAIT requirements is to find a file located somewhere on the computer. The file may be in a folder or subfolder on the hard disk, or it may be on a different drive.

Some releases of Windows use Find on the Start menu, rather than Search.

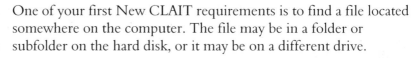

1 Select Start, Search. This displays the Search Results window. On the left is the Search Companion pane which guides you through the process.

Winlogo+F will start the Search for Files or Folders whatever your activity.

2 You could decide to search for All files and folders. However, the CLAIT file will be a text file, so select Documents.

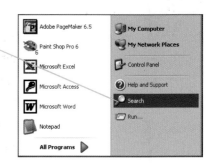

*You can substitute wild cards, ? and *, for all or part of the file name. The ? replaces an individual character in that position, the * represents all characters. For example, in the Search box, *.doc would find all the files in the search area that matched the Word .doc file extension.*

3 You now have the option to narrow the search by specifying a time period for the 'Last time it was modified' (this includes created). 'Don't remember' is the default.

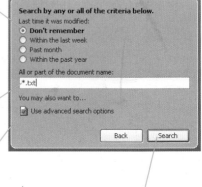

If you realise that you have made a mistake, or you can see the file you want, you can stop the search.

4 Type in the file name if you know it, or *.txt if you don't know the full name, but know it is a text file. You can use the Advanced search options, which allow you to include a word or phrase that was in the document. Click Search when ready.

The list of files that match your search criteria will be displayed in the right hand pane. You will find it useful to maximise the window.

If your search completes with no files to display, check your file name and search criteria.

5 If you have found the required file, select Yes, finished searching. The search facility closes leaving the results.

6 It's a good idea to sort the results if there are many. Click the button to expand and view the options. Sorting by name arranges them alphabetically. Sorting by date puts the newest files at the end of the list.

7 You can also select to view the results with details. This provides the date and time stamp. The Thumbnails view is useful if you are looking for an image file.

Most data file types are associated with an application. Part of the installation process for software involves telling Windows which file types use the application. When you double click a file in the Search Result, or in Windows Explorer or in folders view, Windows associates that file type with an application and will open that file in the correct software.

8 With a great number of files you may decide to refine the search. You can supply a more precise file name, or limit the search location.

9 When you have found the required file, double click it, and it will open in the appropriate application.

Open a file with the application

You can use the Open file function in all applications to look for a file. Explorer showed how folders can be organised, and in the Windows Search function, we saw how to change the target search area. The Open file function allows us to use similar features.

All applications apply filters to the Open and Save windows. This means that you will see the normal file type for that application. If the file you want is not visible, check that you have opened the correct application.

1 In Word, select File, Open, or click on the Open folder button. The Open window lists files in the current folder. Because Word is our sample application, it will initially show subfolders and .doc files.

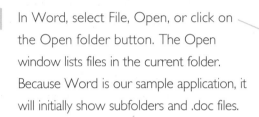

You will need to click the down arrow in the Files of type box. Select All Files (*.*) or Text Files, (*.txt) to narrow the search. This will then list any text files in the selected drive or folder.

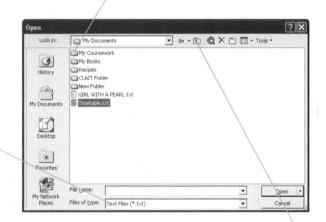

You can use the navigation buttons in the left panel to go straight to the folders listed.

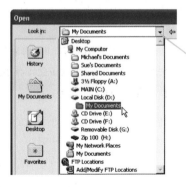

2 You can select the Up One Level button to go to the parent folder. You can also click in the Look in box to get the menu of other possible locations. Click on the drive or folder you want.

3 When you see the required file, select it and click Open, or double click on its icon.

Editing a file

With the document open in the application, you can review the contents and add the text as required.

Word processing is dealt with extensively in the next unit. See page 30 for more help.

1 The application that opens will be a text editor, in our example it is Word. Notice how the Word window shares many of the same features as the folder window shown previously.

2 The Title bar shows the file name and the application name.

3 The mouse symbol is currently an I beam. It will change to a pointer as you move it to the edge of the screen.

You are only required to type a very small amount of text in this unit. It is essential that it is 100% correct, including spacing and capitalisation.

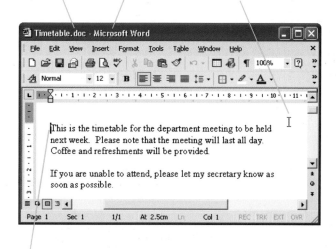

4 The typing cursor (the vertical flashing bar) will be in the top left of the screen. To move the cursor, click with the mouse where you want to start typing. Alternatively, you can use the arrows on the keyboard.

5 To insert blank lines, position the cursor at the end of the text and press the Enter key a few times. Then type the text.

Saving the file

Office applications are designed to save a file with the original name and in the original folder or drive location. Because the file already has a name, when you select Save, you will not be prompted for a file name. The existing copy of the file will be automatically overwritten.

When you change and save an existing file, the original will be replaced.

1 Select File, Save, or click on the diskette symbol in the Toolbar.

2 The file will be saved but there will be little apparent activity unless you are saving to the floppy disk. You may see a rapidly shrinking box or get a message in the Status bar at the bottom of the screen.

You can customise the Standard Toolbar to include Save As, but there is no standard button.

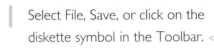

3 To save the file with a different name, select File, Save As.

Whilst the file name is highlighted in blue, you can just type the new file name, and the current name disappears.

4 Change the file name and check the destination folder, press Save.

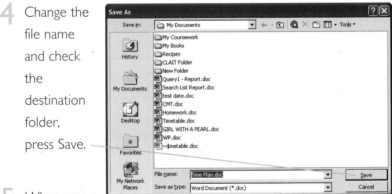

You can choose to save a file as another type, but with certain restrictions.
Picture files have many different formats, and there are advantages in the differences. Click in the Save as type box to view the options.

5 When you save a new file, the Save As process is automatically invoked. The .doc three letter file extension identifies the file as a Word document and is added automatically.

Printing

All you need to know for New CLAIT is how to switch on the printer, load paper and use the standard default settings to print your documents.

To see which printers are attached to your computer, select Start, Control Panel, Printers and Faxes. This opens the Printers folder.

1   In this folder you will see the Printer Tasks frame with printing controls. Add a Printer starts the wizard which guides you through the installation process.

You can use Task bar settings to add the printers folder directly to the Start menu.

2   You may find more than one printer installed on your computer. You can have both local printers and network printers. The default printer is indicated by a tick symbol on its icon.

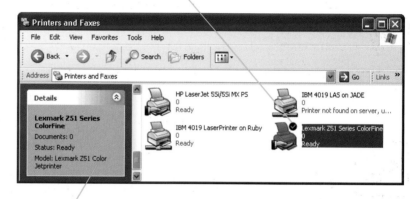

Open Printer properties, click the Paper tab, and check that the paper size is set to A4 in the UK.

3   The Details frame shows the status of the selected printer. For more information, select the printer, right click and choose Properties.

To print in WordPad, you can click on the Printer button, shown on the Toolbar. To print in NotePad, select File, Print from the menu. See page 42 for details on printing in Word.

4   When you select print in an application, the printer icon will appear in the System Tray on the desktop. This provides you with a shortcut to the printer that is only available whilst the printer is active.

Managing the printer

Printing is a three stage process. The document is formatted by the application. The results are passed to a holding area, known as the print spool. Then the information is transferred progressively to the printer. If it is just a brief text document, it will probably print before you are able to cancel. With longer documents or pictures, however, it is possible to pause or cancel the print.

Make sure that you take an opportunity, before the Unit exam, to learn how to switch the printer on and load paper as these are requirements of the course.

1 Double click the printer icon in the System Tray to open the printer folder. Click the button to expand Printer Tasks.

2 To pause a document, select Pause printing. The option changes to Resume printing.

3 To see which documents are still waiting to be printed, select See what's printing. This opens the printer window and displays the list of files.

It's best to avoid turning the printer off whilst it is printing.

4 To cancel the print, select the file, and from the menu bar select Document, Cancel.

If you are using a network printer, you may find it slow to respond to instructions to pause or cancel.

5 If the printer is switched off, or out of paper you will get a warning message. When you switch on or load paper, the printer may well start to print without further action as it is usually set to retry automatically.

Closing

The Taskbar shows which applications you have open. Click on the application name and it will list the names of any files you may have open. You can close the individual file, but leave the application open.

You can right click a file on the Taskbar and select close from that menu. If the file has been modified it will ask if you wish to save.

I   Click on the lower Close Window button on the right of the window, or select File, Close.

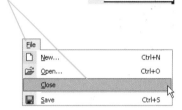

2   If you have not already saved the file, or if you have made any changes since the last save, you will be prompted to save now.

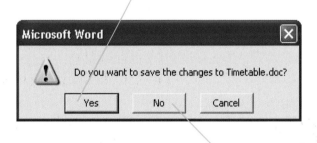

3   If you wish to discard the changes, then click No. Any alterations made will be lost.

If you are working on a floppy disk, then you must close those files before you remove the disk. Otherwise, the application will prompt you to re-insert the disk before it will close.

4   When you want to close the application completely, select File, Exit, or click on the Close button at the top right of the screen.

5   If you have several files open, hold down the shift key when you click File. Select Close All from the menu. You will be prompted to save any changed files.

Shutdown

When you have finished working, it is very important that you close down the computer properly. While you have been working, the operating system has been running in the background, managing memory usage and the storage of files. When you use the correct closing procedure, Windows is able to ensure that all the temporary files it has created are erased and its own system files are closed.

If you turn off the computer without using the correct Shut Down procedure, you will find that the next time you turn on the computer, the ScanDisk program will run to check out the system.

1 Check the Taskbar and ensure that all the applications you have been using are now closed.

2 Click the Start button. As separate Users have been defined one User can Log Off, and allow

another User to Log On, without closing down the system.

Occasionally you may find that the system freezes and stops responding to the keyboard or mouse. Press Ctrl+Alt+Del simultaneously on the keyboard. This will bring up the Close Program window, and will indicate which program is not responding. You may then be able to close just that program and continue working.

3 Select Turn Off Computer. From the next window you can choose Stand By mode. This allows you to leave the computer switched on but reduce the power consumption. When you return it remembers exactly where you were and you can carry on using the same applications.

4 Restart means you can close down and restart the computer without actually turning it off.

When the Shut Down process is complete, you will get the message 'It is now safe to turn off the computer'.

5 Select Turn Off. Some computers power off automatically, you will not need to switch them off physically. If this happens, the monitor may go into Stand By mode, so you can turn it off independently.

Exercise

Scenario

You have been moved to the computing facility at Surprise Gardens. Complete the following exercise to show that you are able to use a computer.

The computer is set up ready for you to use. You may need a password to gain access to the data.

1. Switch on the computer and monitor correctly and safely.

2. Wait for the operating system to fully load.

3. Using the operating system's facility to 'find file' or search, find the file Supplier (or Supplier.txt if your system shows file types).

4. Using an application that will allow you to read the file, open the file Supplier.

5. Using the mouse and keyboard add your name, exam centre number and today's date at the end of the document.

6. Save the document using the original file name Supplier.

7. Switch on the printer, and load a few sheets of paper.

8. Print the document using the default settings.

9. Close the document.

10. Create a new text document using the same software.

11. Enter the following as shown, leaving a blank line between each line of text:
    45 kg of bulbs @ £1.75
    Part no. G246: 10% increase
    Your name, your exam centre number and today's date

12. Save this document using the file name Practical.

13. Print the document using the default settings.

14. Close the document.

15. Exit the application correctly and shut down the operating system.

Checklist

When you have finished the exercise, use the following checklist. Have you:

- Opened the correct file
- Entered the text as required, in the right place
- Saved the file using exactly the same file name
- Printed the file and closed it
- Created a new document using the same application
- Entered the text, exactly as specified
- Saved the file using the specified file name
- Printed and closed the file
- Closed the application and shut down the computer

Answers

Print 1

Surprise Garden Centres Supplier

There has been a change to one of our suppliers of summer bulbs, tubers and corms.

These later flowering plants such as lilies and Agapanthus will now be coming from a new centre in the Channel Islands. They will be available starting in mid March.

For further information please contact Julie on ext 2414.

Sue Price Centre No 12345   17th August 2002

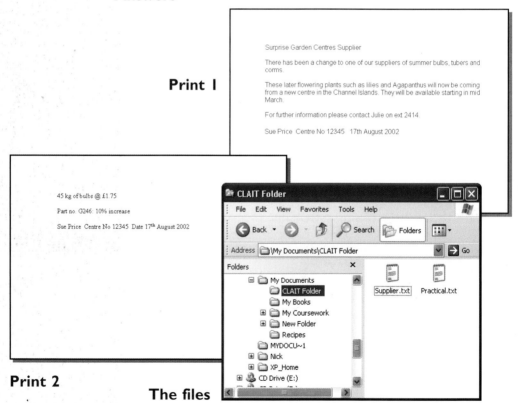

45 kg of bulbs @ £1.75

Part no. G246: 10% increase

Sue Price Centre No 12345 Date 17th August 2002

Print 2

The files

Word processing

This unit is designed to introduce the basics of word processing. It shows how to create a short document, edit and format the text, manage the document layout, save the file and print the document.

Covers

Unit Two

Word processing

If you look at your text files in the folder or Explorer view, you will see that Notepad uses the .txt file extension, while Word uses the .doc file extension.

A word processor and a text editor each allow us to input and manipulate text. However, they do have different roles and capabilities. Notepad, for example, is a plain text editor that comes with Windows. We can use it to move and copy text, but it has limited function in comparison with a full word processor. Notepad is useful because the text has no formatting and can be used by almost any application.

Microsoft Word, on the other hand, formats text so that its files can only be read in applications that understand the Word file format, particularly the Office suite of programs. If you wish to transfer the text to other applications, you may need to strip out any formatting, and save it as a text file.

We need to use a full word processor, such as Word, for the New CLAIT course as we are required to use formatting to emphasise and align text, set margins and manage the document layout. We are also able to use word processing tools such as the spell check program, to ensure that we complete the task successfully.

Word makes formatting text easy, but more than that, it actually shows us how the text will appear on the page. It is known as a WYSIWYG program -What You See Is What You Get. It allows us to evaluate the formatting and layout we have chosen. When working through the New CLAIT exercises, we can check that we have fulfilled the requirements, e.g. make the heading bold.

These pictures illustrate the same text, as a Notepad text file without formatting, and as a Word document with formatting.

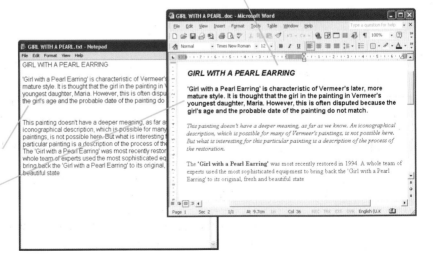

You only need to click the mouse on the Start button, and on the Microsoft Word entry.

Press Start, All Programs, Microsoft Word. This displays the main Word window, showing a blank document screen, ready for you to start typing.

Parts of the Word window:

See page 20 to open an existing file.

Menu bar   Title bar   Word's Help facilities

Standard toolbar   Formatting toolbar   Task Pane

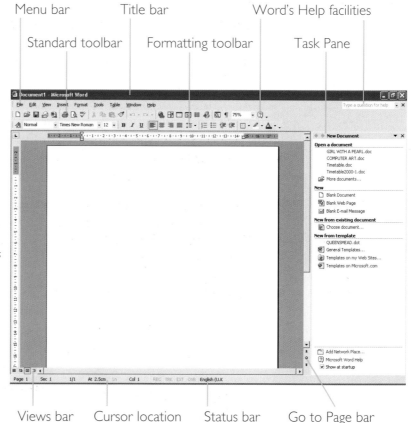

Take note of the names of the various bars, such as Standard toolbar and Status bar as they will be frequently referred to throughout the unit.

Views bar   Cursor location   Status bar   Go to Page bar

If you want to start a second document, click the New Blank Document button on the toolbar. The Title bar will now show Document2. You can have several documents open at once.

The standard Word window gives us a great deal of information. As you become familiar with the details shown on the screen, it becomes much easier to use the program facilities and to troubleshoot problems.

Remember to check the Windows Taskbar as well. This shows you how many documents you have open.

Optimise your view

You can easily change the view from Normal to Print layout, so use the view that you are most comfortable with.

Word provides you with several ways to see your document as you work. You can select the style of window and manage features that are available to suit your own preferences.

1 Normal view lets you see the maximum typing area. Print Layout view shows you the text as it will appear on the paper, including margin area. To change views select View from the menu bar.

It is a good idea to adjust your view of the typing page so that you can see as much text at once as possible.

2 You can also change views by selecting the view you want from the Views bar at the bottom of the screen.

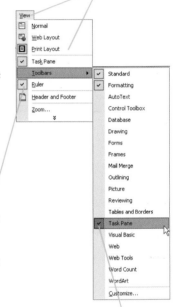

Standard and Formatting toolbars are accessed through the View, Toolbars option.

3 Also using the View menu, you can select to show the ruler at the top of the typing area. The ruler shows you the typing width that you are using. Initially, this may not seem important, but later in the CLAIT exercise you will be asked to change the width of the margins. From the ruler you can see the associated change in the typing width.

The ruler always starts at zero, whichever view you use. The margins themselves are not included in the measurement.

4 On the previous page we saw the Word window with the Task Pane showing, You can choose to have the task pane open or closed by selecting it from the View menu. The presence of a tick indicates that the task pane is active. Clicking the entry again removes the tick (and removes the Task Pane from the list of toolbars).

Even if you have a version of Word that does not have a Task Pane, the functions are still available through the menus and toolbars.

5 The relevant Task Pane appears automatically when you perform certain activities, such as cut and paste or inserting Clip Art. Each task pane presents you with a group of activities, and the option to view other panes.

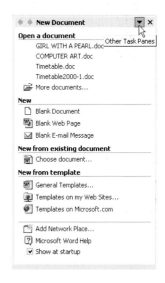

6 The Word window on page 31 also shows the Standard and Formatting toolbars, each on a separate row. To make them share the same row, and free up more viewable typing area, select View, Toolbars, Customise, select the Options tab.

If you wish, you can choose to show shortcut keys in the ScreenTips. This is a good way to become familiar with the keyboard shortcuts.

7 You will also see on this menu that you can select large icons.

8 The Show ScreenTips option, selected here, tells you the purpose of the buttons on the toolbars when you hover the mouse over them, a useful feature if you find the buttons difficult to interpret.

9 One other item that may help with your view of the Word window, is the zoom level. You can select an entry from the drop down list, or you can experiment with typing a percentage into the box.

Margins and spacing

Once you have opened Word, and have your window ready for typing, the next requirement is to set the page margins. You will find that the left and right margins are already set at a default value of either 2.54 or 3.17 cms (1 or 1.5 inches).

Margins are set for a whole page. If you want to indent just a single paragraph, then use Format, Paragraph, Indents and Spacing.

1 Select File, Page Setup.

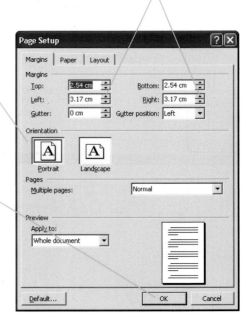

2 Make sure the Margins tab on the Page Setup dialog box is selected.

The most recently-used tab in a dialog box, is the one that will be foremost when you reopen the dialog box.

3 You are required to change the left and right margins. The top and bottom margins are seldom changed.

4 The amount shown is the default setting. Type into the box the amount you require, or use the up and down arrows.

5 Note that the Page Setup dialog box also allows you to change the orientation of your paper from portrait to landscape.

6 Click the OK button. When you return to the document, you will find the typing width shown on the horizontal ruler has changed.

It's worth considering learning to touch type. You can work so much faster, and it looks very professional! Have a look on the Web for tutorials.

Now you are ready to type. As you type, the cursor or printing point, will travel across the screen. Continue typing even when you reach the right-side edge and the text will wrap onto the next line. When you reach the end of the paragraph, press Enter. Press Enter again for another blank line, and continue with the next paragraph.

There are certain accepted standards in typing, and the New CLAIT course adheres to them.

- one blank space between words
- one blank space after a comma
- one or two spaces after a full stop, question mark or exclamation mark
- paragraphs must start at the left margin, not be indented even by a single blank
- one clear blank line between paragraphs
- one or two clear blank lines under a heading

You must also make sure that your spacing is correct when you insert, delete, move or copy text.

The New CLAIT course also requires that you type accurately, speed is not important. You must follow all capitalisation as it is shown. You do not need to follow line endings as shown, only paragraph endings.

Creating blank lines

To create a blank line, use the Enter key. To create a break in the middle of a paragraph, put the cursor just before the first letter of the new paragraph, and press Enter twice. The first Enter splits the paragraph, the second Enter gives the clear blank line between the paragraphs.

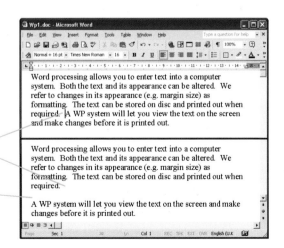

Editing text

Insert and overtype

Word has two typing modes, insert and overtype. Normally when you open Word it is set to insert mode, which means that if you wish to insert another word in the middle of some text, you just position the cursor where you want the word, and type. The text to the right will be pushed along, and where necessary will automatically wrap onto the next line.

If you press the Insert key on the keyboard, it switches to Overtype mode, and any words that you type will replace the existing text.

Delete text

For individual letters or small amounts of text, you can use the backspace or delete keys as appropriate – it just depends where the cursor is in relation to the text you wish to edit.

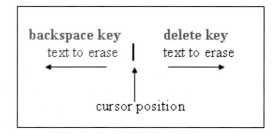

When you wish to delete sentences or larger amounts of text, select the text first and press the delete key. For more information on selecting text see page 43.

The backspace and delete key will remove blank lines, or part blank lines. If the cursor is at the left margin or at the end of a paragraph, press delete and the following blank line or lines will be removed. If the cursor is at the beginning of the next paragraph, press backspace, and blank lines above the cursor will be removed.

Show/hide

The Show/hide button reveals spaces, tabs and paragraph symbols (Enter key). Use this feature to make sure that you have the correct spacing between words, and that you have not pressed Enter at the right margin, but allowed the text to wrap automatically.

The show/Hide facility is especially useful when editing fully justified text, as it is difficult to check the spacing between words.

Tab   Spaces   Paragraph symbol

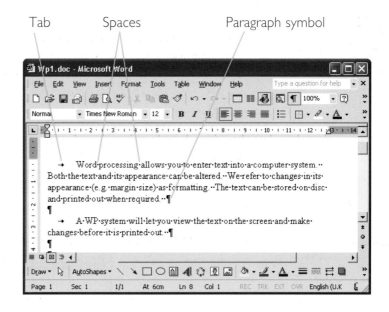

The Undo facility

As you work Word keeps a running log of your actions. This means that if you wish, you can actually reverse or undo the action. Once you have Undone an action, you can then also Redo the action. Word continues to log your actions until you close the file.

You cannot undo saving a file. If you wish to keep the original version, you must use Save As and give the file a different name.

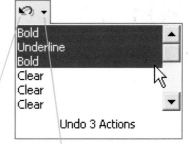

1   You can select Edit, Undo from the menu, or click on the Undo button.

2   If you wish to undo a series of actions, then click on the down arrow next to the Undo symbol. You can only undo actions in the same sequence in which they were executed.

3   When you close the document, the record of actions is discarded and you start afresh.

The Spell Checker

Press the F7 Function key to invoke the Spell Checker.

The spell check program is normally enabled when you start Word. You will find that any misspelled words are underlined in red, and grammatical or spacing errors are underlined in green. When you are ready to make the corrections:

1 Select Tools, Spelling or Grammar, or click on the button.

Make sure that the Spell check dictionary is set to UK English. You may find that it is set to ignore words in capitals or words with numbers, so you should check these carefully.

2 The misspelled word will be shown in red, with the suggestion(s) for the correction in the lower pane.

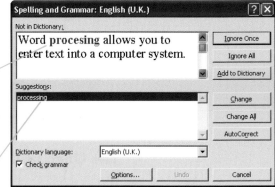

The Grammar check will make suggestions for alternative wording. It is important that you copy the text as shown in the exercise and ignore any grammar changes. However it is useful to identify extra spaces between words and punctuation errors.

3 Select the Change button, if you wish, and the spell checker will automatically move to the next misspelled word

4 You can add the word to the dictionary (Add to Dictionary button), a good idea if it is frequently used, such as the name of your town, or a technical term.

5 Word will tell you when the check is complete.

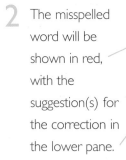

There is no substitute for proof reading. The Spell Checker will not find words that are spelled correctly but out of context, such as 'through' instead of 'threw', or 'the' instead of 'they'.

6 If you wish you can spell check words individually as you type. Click with the right mouse button on the word, and you will be given the spelling suggestions immediately.

Save your document

When you have typed in your text, and even at some point before you have finished, you should save your document. You may find that Word does an autosave at set intervals, but you still need to formally save your document with a name.

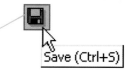

I Press Ctrl+S, or select File, Save or click on the diskette button.

More detail on navigating folders when you save files is given in Unit 1, Using a Computer, see page 22.

2 The Save As dialog box appears as the file has not yet been saved and has no name or defined location.

3 Check the Save in folder name. If you wish to save it to a different drive or folder, select it now.

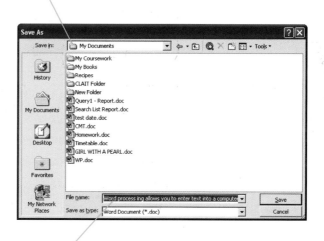

4 Word has used the first line of the document as the file name. You could accept the name and just click on Save. However, as the name is so long, it would be sensible to abbreviate or amend it.

5 If you wish to abbreviate it, click in the bar and use the normal editing keys. If you wish to type a name, just type - the text highlighted in blue will just disappear. Then press Save.

Save with the same file name

It's a good idea to save the file frequently. Once the file has a name and folder or drive location you can simply press Ctrl+S, or click on the diskette symbol as shown on the previous page. This will overwrite the original file with the additional or amended data.

Save with new file name

As part of the New CLAIT word processing unit, when you have amended your document you are required to save it with a different name. We must use the Save As function to achieve this.

Press the F12 Function key to take you straight into the Save As command.

1 Select File, Save As. There is no toolbar button for this function.

File	
Open...	Ctrl+O
Close	
Save	Ctrl+S
Save As...	
Page Setup...	
Print Preview	
Print...	Ctrl+P
1 C:\Oasthse\beginner\Disk\Wp1.doc	
2 D:\My Documents\Homework.doc	
3 D:\My Documents\WP.doc	
4 D:\My Documents\GIRL WITH A PEARL.doc	
Acquire Text...	
Acquire Text Settings...	
Exit	

2 The Save As dialog box that appears is as shown on the previous page.

3 Amend the name, as required. Remember, if the file name is highlighted in blue, it will disappear when you begin to type. If you click in the file name box, the highlight disappears but leaves the existing name for you to amend.

4 Make sure you save the file with the name exactly as specified in the exercise, with no extra blanks or characters, as this is also marked.

You may also use the Save As command to save a copy of a file to a different location.

See page 30 for more information on text files.

Save as new file type

You can use the Save or Save As commands to save the file as a different type, if for example you wished to transfer the file to a text editor. However, for the New CLAIT exercises this should be avoided, since the file will lose formatting.

Print preview

The Print Preview function is a valuable tool. It not only will save you paper, but also time.

1 Select Print Preview on the toolbar.

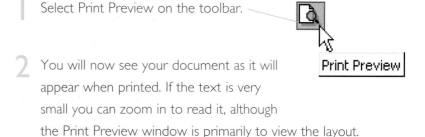

2 You will now see your document as it will appear when printed. If the text is very small you can zoom in to read it, although the Print Preview window is primarily to view the layout.

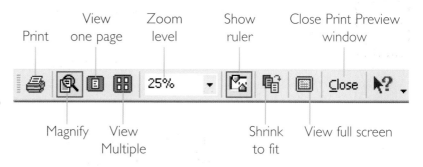

Print   View one page   Zoom level   Show ruler   Close Print Preview window

Magnify   View Multiple   Shrink to fit   View full screen

3 Selecting the Print button will bypass the Print dialog box and start the printing process immediately. View Multiple Pages lets you see up to fifteen pages at once, or use the Next and Previous Page buttons to scroll through the document. Click with the mouse anywhere on the text to zoom in and out on the text.

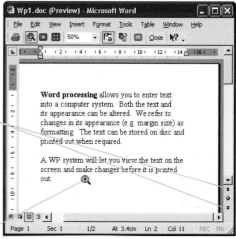

Print your file

Most New CLAIT exercises only require you to print one page.

You can print your file directly from the Print Preview window, or by clicking on the Printer button, but to control the printing process, and change any of the defaults, such as the printer, you need to use the Print Dialog box.

You can check to see if your printer is set to use A4 paper by clicking the Properties button.

1 To open the Print dialog box, select File, Print.

2 If you have more than one printer attached, select the printer.

If you want to print one page only, position the cursor somewhere on the page you want and select to print current page.

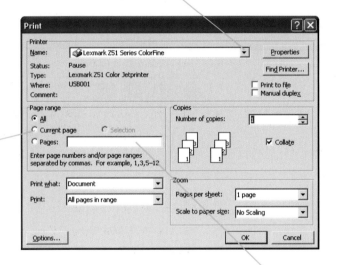

Printing and managing your printer are also covered in Using a Computer. See page 23-24.

3 The set option is to print the whole document. You may wish to print only certain pages. Click in the Pages button, and type your selection. For individual pages, type the page numbers separated by commas, e.g. 2,5,8. For consecutive pages separate them with a hyphen, e.g. 2-8.

4 Other options include specifying number of copies and how many pages per sheet. When you have completed your selection, click OK and the printing will start.

Select text

Before looking at text formatting (see page 44), you should first become familiar with selecting portions of text. When text is selected it is shown in reverse video, or highlighted, ready for you to perform actions to change its appearance etc. There are several ways to select text:

Double click a word to select just the word.

Ctrl+A selects everything in the document.

1 To select a whole line, such as a title, position the mouse arrow in the left margin, so it is pointing at the text, then click with the left mouse button.

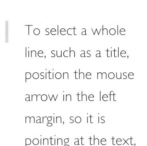
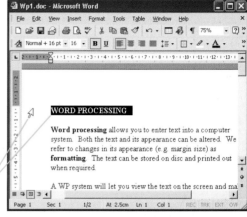

2 To select several lines or a whole paragraph, position the cursor in the left margin, at the beginning of the text. Click and drag down, or up, staying in the left margin.

3 To select text in the middle of a paragraph, click at the beginning of the text, hold down the Shift key and click at the end of the required text.

4 For individual words, or if you find controlling the mouse difficult, you can use the keyboard. Position the cursor at the beginning of the required text and hold down the Shift key while you press the arrow keys. You can also use the Home and End keys.

Use Shift and the arrow keys to select text that extends beyond the top or bottom boundaries of the screen. It gives you much more control and you can continue to select text one line at a time, that would otherwise be out of sight.

5 To remove the highlight, just click anywhere that is not highlighted.

Format text

See page 32 for instructions on how to view the Formatting toolbar.

Formatting text means changing the way it appears on the page. It may for example be underlined, italicised or made larger. You can apply formatting to the text once you have finished typing, or you can initiate a format change so that the new formatting appears as you type.

To apply colour, select the text and click on the button. To select a different colour, click on the down arrow.

1 To change the font style and size, select the text you wish to alter. The current font style is Times New Roman. Click the down arrow to view alternatives, and click on your choice. See page 136 for more information on font types.

In the CLAIT exercise, when you are asked to change the font on a specified section of text, make sure that the font is obviously different.

Font style   Font type   Font size

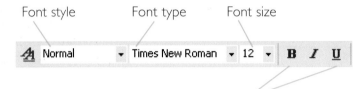

2 Bold, Italic and Underline are toggle switches. Select the text and click on one or a combination of the buttons. If you wish to remove an effect, re-select the text and click that format button again.

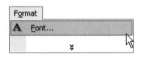

The Format painter allows you to copy the format from one piece of text to another. Position the cursor in the required formatted text. Single click the button to apply formatting once, double click to apply formatting several times. Click the button again when finished.

3 Select Format, Font from the menu bar to view the full range of formats that you can apply. You can select the underline style, subscript and superscript. The Preview panel shows the effect of the format change.

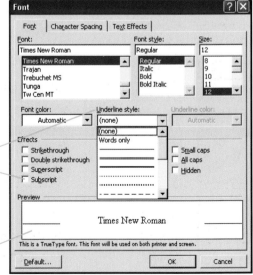

Alignment and line spacing

Text can be aligned in four ways:

Left aligned –   the text is straight at the left margin and ragged on the right margin. This is how text will be normally aligned when you open Word.

Centred –   when you centre text using the centre function, the text stays centred even when you change the margin width.

Right aligned –   the text is straight at the right margin, ragged at the left. This is mainly used for addresses at the head of letters.

Justified –   the text is straight at both margins. To achieve this Word has to stretch the spaces between the text. Therefore it sometimes appears that you have more than one space between words.

Use the Show/ hide button to check the spacing between words when you specify fully justified text (see page 36).

left align (currently selected)   right align   line spacing

centre

justified

	1.0
	1.5
	2.0
	2.5
	3.0
	More...

1   To change the alignment, just position the cursor in the line or paragraph, and click on the button of choice.

When you select the whole document and change the alignment, you will find that centred titles become left aligned.

2   The alignment buttons are not toggle switches. To reset or change to another layout you must make another selection.

3   You can use Ctrl+A to select the whole document and then use the alignment button.

If this button is not available, select Format, Paragraph. You can specify Line spacing on the Indents and Spacing tab.

4   For line spacing, again, just position the cursor in the paragraph and select from the list. Choosing More takes you to the Format Paragraph dialog box, where you can specify your own.

Move and copy text

To move text from one position to another:

Page 43 describes the various ways provided for selecting the text you wish to move or copy.

1 Select or highlight the text you want to move. Remember to check the spacing at the beginning or end of the text you have selected. You must make sure that the spacing that is left when you remove the text is correct.

2 Click on the Cut button to 'cut' the text from the page, or you can select Edit, Cut from the menu bar. The selected text will disappear and the remaining text will realign itself to fill the space.

The keyboard shortcut for Cut is Ctrl+X. The text you remove is placed in the Clipboard area (see page 47).

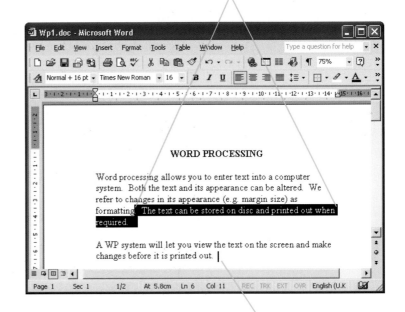

When you cut and paste text, check to make sure that your text still wraps correctly at the right margin.

3 Position the cursor where you wish to insert the text. Make sure that the cursor is flashing as a normal vertical bar.

4 Use Edit, Paste or click on the Paste button. The text will be inserted at the cursor point, and the existing text will be realigned to make space. Again, check the spacing to make sure it is correct.

To copy text, use a similar procedure:

I Select the text and click on the Copy button. This time the text stays in place, and it looks like nothing has happened. However, a copy of the selected text has been placed in the Clipboard and the Paste button is now activated.

2 Position the cursor where you wish to place a copy of the text, and click on the Paste button.

The Clipboard

To move and copy text, the computer uses the Clipboard facility. This is a utility that holds information in memory until the computer is shut down. The data that you have selected to cut or copy, can be reused in the same application, or it can be transferred to another.

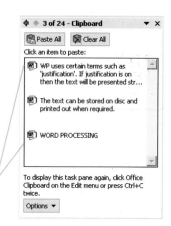

You can manage data in the Clipboard by viewing the Clipboard task pane.

3 Position the cursor in the document where you wish to paste the text. Then click on the item in the task pane that you require. The text will be inserted immediately.

4 A Clipboard Smart Tag will appear below the pasted text. Click on the down arrow to view the options. When you continue typing the tag disappears.

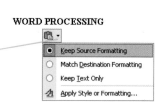

Find and replace

As part of the CLAIT exercise, you will be required to replace a particular word, using the Find and Replace function.

The Find and Replace commands are less used, so may not appear when you first click on Edit. Wait for the full Edit menu to appear, or click on the symbol at the bottom of the list.

1 From the menu, select Edit, Replace. This takes you to the same dialog box as the Find command, but the Replace tab will be foremost.

2 In the Find what box, type in the appropriate word. Word will look for all forms of the target word so you do not need to be concerned about capitalisation.

When you click on the More button, it changes to a Less button. This allows you to see more of your document as it is searched.

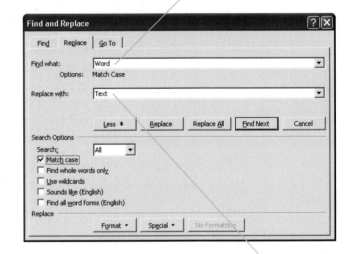

Only select Match case if you wish to limit the search to capitalised words.

It is a good idea to avoid Replace All until you see how the Replace function is working, especially in older versions of Word, where capitalisation is treated differently.

3 You can then press the Tab key, or click in the Replace with box and type the replacing word. If you type without capitals, Word will capitalise the replacing word as appropriate.

4 Click on the Find next button. If you do not wish to replace the word, click again on Find next. If you do wish to replace the word, click on Replace and Word will automatically move to the next occurrence.

Close the file, exit Word

When you have finished all the editing required in the document, save the file with the file name as specified. To close the file:

1 From the menu, select File, Close or click on the Close file button.

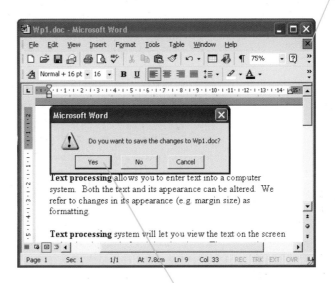

When prompted to save the document on closing, if you select Yes to save, it will overwrite the original without further checking.

2 If you have omitted to save the file before closing, you will be prompted to do so now. However, you will need to press Cancel and select the Save As function if you you want to save the document under a different file name.

If you select File, New you are presented with options for different Word templates by the New Document task pane. If you click on the New blank document button, you get the standard document format.

3 When you have closed all other open Word documents, you can select File, Exit, or click on the Close button on the title bar.

4 You can close the documents but leave the application running. It will be shown on the task bar. If you have Word open but no documents, the main typing area will be shown in grey, and most of the buttons will not function.

Exercise

Scenario

Your manager has asked you create a report for the local gardening club.

1.   Create a new word processing document.

2.   Set the left and right page margins to 3 cms.

3.   Enter the following text with an unjustified right margin and a justified left margin.

Gardening Today

Gardening has become a very popular hobby. Many thousands of people in this country take a great interest in it, and many hours of television and radio are devoted to this hobby.

As a result of this popularity, garden centres have sprung up everywhere. These centres sell a wide range of items, from plants and water features to garden furniture, barbecues and spa pools. Many now serve coffee and meals, so that a visit to a garden centre can become a real day out.

For the modern gardener, these garden centres can provide 'instant' gardens. They display garden structures and water features as they might look in your own garden. The plants that these garden centres generally provide are the more popular annual or perennial plants, usually in bloom, so that the purchaser can see both the colour and overall effect of the plant.

Those for whom gardening is more than just a hobby, will usually find that they have to visit or get catalogues from the smaller, specialist nurseries.

4.   Enter your name, centre number and today's date a few lines below the end of the text.

5.   Format the heading so that it is larger than the rest of the text.

6.   Save your report with the filename Gardening and print one copy.

Your manager has asked for the following amendments to be made to the report.

7. Insert a paragraph break and clear linespace in the third paragraph after the words ….in your own garden.

8. Delete the last sentence of the second paragraph.

    Many now serve coffee and meals, so that a visit to a garden centre can become a real day out.

9. Move the first sentence of the second paragraph

    As a result of this popularity, garden centres have sprung up everywhere.

    so that it becomes the last sentence of the first paragraph.

10. Insert the following text as the final sentence of the second paragraph, after the words …barbeques and spa pools.

    Many also carry a wide range of gazebos and conservatories.

11. Replace all occurrences of hobby with pastime (three times in all).

12. Change only the heading Gardening Today to a different font.

13. Embolden and centre the heading Gardening Today. Ensure the rest of the text in not emboldened.

14. Fully justify all the text apart from the heading.

15. Change the left and right margins to 4 cms.

16. Set the second paragraph only in double line spacing.

17. Save the report with the new filename Gardening Today.

18. Print a final copy of the report.

19. Close the document and exit the application correctly.

Checklist

When you have finished the exercise, use the following checklist.
Have you:

Errors mainly arise from not reading the questions properly, missing a step or requirement, or failing to proof-read thoroughly. Always check your final printout as mistakes are much more evident on paper.

- Created and saved the document with the correct file names
- Entered and proof read all the text
- Set and modified the margins to the correct sizes
- Aligned and modified the alignment of text, including the title
- Used a larger font and different font where required
- Used formatting to emphasise text
- Inserted, deleted, replaced and moved the specified text
- Printed the document when requested

Answers

Gardening Today

Gardening has become a very popular hobby. Many thousands of people in this country take a great interest in it, and many hours of television and radio are devoted to this hobby.

As a result of this popularity, garden centres have sprung up everywhere. These centres sell a wide range of items, from plants and water features to garden furniture, barbeques and spa pools. Many now serve coffee and meals, so that a visit to a garden centre can become a real day out.

For the modern gardener, these garden centres can provide 'instant' gardens. They display garden structures and water features as they might look in your own garden. The plants that these garden centres generally provide are the more popular annual or perennial plants, usually in bloom, so that the purchaser can see both the colour and overall effect of the plant.

Those for whom gardening is more than just a hobby, will usually find that they have to visit or get catalogues from the smaller, specialist nurseries.

Sue Price
Centre No:
Date:

Print 1

GARDENING TODAY

Gardening has become a very popular pastime. Many thousands of people in this country take a great interest in it, and many hours of television and radio are devoted to this pastime. As a result of this popularity, garden centres have sprung up everywhere.

These centres sell a wide range of items, from plants and

water features to garden furniture, barbeques and spa

pools. Many also carry a wide range of gazebos and

conservatories.

For the modern gardener, these garden centres can provide 'instant' gardens. They display garden structures and water features as they might look in your own garden.

The plants that these garden centres generally provide are the more popular annual or perennial plants, usually in bloom, so that the purchaser can see both the colour and overall effect of the plant.

Those for whom gardening is more than just a pastime, will usually find that they have to visit or get catalogues from the smaller, specialist nurseries.

Sue Price
Centre No:
Date:

Print 2

Electronic communication

This unit covers the two basics of electronic communication, e-mail and the Internet. The e-mail component includes sending, receiving, forwarding mail, using attachments and the address book. The Internet element includes searching the Web and managing the results.

Covers

Unit Three

E-mail and the Internet

We have separated e-mail and the Internet for function and software purposes. However, to use e-mail you still need to connect through a network, whether it is a local area network (LAN), a wide area network (Wan), or the Internet.

For the purpose of the New CLAIT course, electronic communication can be divided into two categories – communication between individuals and communication to a general audience. E-mail is used to send information between friends, family, business contacts etc., in other words, between individuals. The Internet, or World Wide Web is used to make information available to anyone.

E-mail

E-mail stands for electronic mail. It uses telephone and computer connections and can be extremely swift and inexpensive. You can communicate with someone the other side of the world within minutes, at a fraction of the cost of an international telephone call, and much faster than regular mail.

The application we are using for e-mail is Outlook Express, which has e-mail as its main function. It is also possible to use Outlook –

the e-mail part of Outlook is very similar to Outlook Express, as the name would suggest. However, Outlook is also a time management system. It includes a calendar, notes, messages and tasks. It has greater function than needed for this course but can be used in the same way to complete the exercises.

Outlook Express is a PC based e-mail system. This means that you can type and save e-mail messages off-line. When you are ready, connect to your Internet Service Provider (ISP) and send the messages. While you are connected, the computer checks for messages that are held for you by your ISP, and downloads them to your computer. You can then disconnect and read them at your leisure. All of this usually only takes a few minutes.

You can sign up for a Hotmail account at an Internet cafe. You don't need your own computer.

Some e-mail systems are Web based, Hotmail for example. You must first connect, then read and create e-mail whilst you are connected. The great advantage of Web-based e-mail is that you can read and send e-mail from anywhere in the world. The messages are stored on the ISP's computer, so you are not using your own storage space.

The Internet

The Internet is an interwoven network of computers, or a Web, all connected via telephones and satellites. The information that is held on the Web is provided by organisations, companies, governments and individuals.

One way to make information available on the Web is to create your own Web pages and upload them to a host computer. Creating your own Web pages is covered in Unit 9. See page 190.

To search for information on the Internet you need to use a browser. There are other browsers in common use, such as Netscape and Opera, but we are going to use Microsoft's Internet Explorer which comes with all versions of Windows.

If you right click the Dial Up connection, you can select to show the connection icon in the notification area (system tray). When you hover the mouse over the icon, you will see your connection rate. You can also use this icon when you want to disconnect.

The connection

To browse the Internet or to send and receive e-mail, you must be signed on to your ISP. The speed of your connection will affect the rate at which you receive information, whether it is e-mail, possibly with attachments, or Web pages. Cable or broadband (ADSL) connections provide the best rates available. To view your connection rate, select My Network Places, then right click and select Properties. Then double click your Dial Up connection. This will show the Status, Duration and speed of your connection.

Start Outlook Express

Outlook Express is a standard entry in the Windows Start menu. Single click to select and open it. The default window that opens is the main view of the application. It provides access to all the activities.

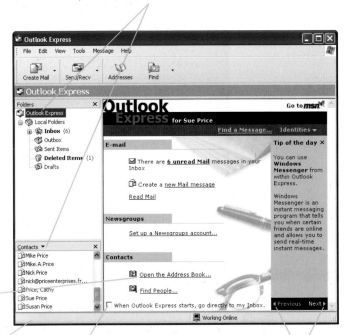

Outlook Express is also included in the Quick Launch bar (if you have this enabled on the task bar), so it is quickly and readily available.

1 If you are using a modem to connect to the Internet, Outlook Express normally starts up Off-line. When you press Send and Receive it will dial up to your ISP.

2 The left pane shows the default view, Outlook Express, with the folders, and contacts.

You can click on any underlined item to go to that activity.

The status bar will tell you if you are in the Online mode.

3 Tick this box to go straight to the Inbox view and bypass this window.

4 You can scroll through Tip of the day to get more useful suggestions.

The Outlook Express Folders

It is important to understand the function of each folder in Outlook Express.

The Inbox – e-mail is downloaded automatically into this folder. It remains here until you read, file or delete it.

The Outbox – when you have created your messages, click on Send. The messages will be transferred to the Outbox and will remain there until you select Send/Receive. If you are working on-line, you can set Outlook Express to perform a Send/Receive automatically at set frequencies. If you are working off-line, select Send/Receive when you have finished and the messages will disappear from the Outbox.

To set your preferences for automatic Send/ Receive, select Tools, Options, and the General tab.

To expand subfolders, click on the + symbol. To collapse subfolders click on the - symbol.

To view the contents of any folder, just click on the folder name in the Folders pane.

In business environments, or where computer disk storage is at a premium, you may find that a copy of the message is not automatically put in the Sent items. Select Tools, Options and the Sent tab to check.

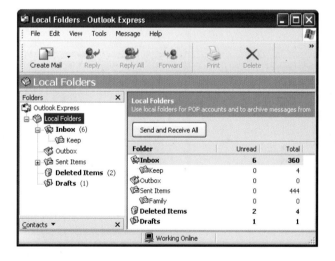

Sent Items – a copy of all the e-mail you have sent is normally transferred to the Sent Items folder.

Deleted Items – when you delete messages, they are sent to this folder, but will remain there until you empty the folder.

Drafts – this is the folder where you can store e-mail that you have created, but not completed, or messages that you do not wish to send at this point.

You can also create your own folders and subfolders (see page 69).

Receive e-mail

The Inbox

When you connect to your ISP, either automatically or by pressing Send/Receive, any messages you have will arrive in the Inbox.

1   You can select the Inbox by clicking in the Folder list. This shows you at a glance how many messages are waiting to be read.

2   The right pane lists the messages that have arrived. Closed envelopes indicate unread messages, also indicated by the bold type. Once read, the envelope shows as open.

You don't have to read unsolicited messages or junk mail if you don't want to. Just select them and press delete.

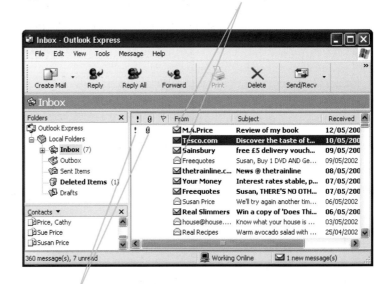

You can customise your view of the Inbox to include a preview pane. It shows the first few lines of the selected message. In effect, this opens the message automatically. This means that you cannot screen your messages, especially for viruses, before you open them.

3   The paper clip indicates that this e-mail has an attachment. The exclamation mark shows that the sender has marked it as priority.

For more information on attachments see page 61.

4   The status bar shows how many messages are in the Inbox, and that there is one new message. You will normally get an audible indication that you have a new message.

5   Double click the message to open it.

The address book

The generic format of an e-mail address is:

userid@mailserveraddress

user name/number   name of the computer
                          storing the user's e-mail

required separator
(pronounced 'at')

Some addresses are case sensitive, so type the e-mail address exactly as given.

To add an address to your address book:

1 Open the message. Click on the name of the sender. Right click and select Add to Address Book.

2 The contact will be added to your address book, and the new entry will appear in the contacts list without any further prompting.

As with many activities in Microsoft Office there is more than one way to add an address to the address book. Just use the method that suits you best.

3 If the contact already exists, you will get a message to that effect.

4 You can add the sender's name to the address book from the message entry in the Inbox. Right click the message and select to Add Sender.

5 In both these methods, only the e-mail address is added to the address book, no other details are completed. Some contacts have more than one e-mail address. To see the e-mail address used, select Properties.

To add an address manually, or to edit and complete details in the address book:

1   Click the Addresses button on the toolbar, visible whichever folder is selected.

2   Select New to add a new address. To change an existing entry, select the contact and click Properties.

3   Complete the details. You will see that you can add Home, Business etc. information. Type in the e-mail address and click Add. The address will be moved to the lower pane and the words Default E-Mail added.

4   The information in the Display box is filled in automatically, and is used in the Contacts pane. You can choose to have surname first if you wish.

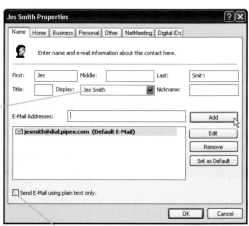

5   If you need to send plain text messages only, click the box. When you have completed the details, select OK. Your new contact will be added to the address book and the contacts pane.

Receive attachments

An attachment can be a document, an image, a spreadsheet or other type of file. An attachment is indicated on the e-mail by the paper clip symbol.

Open the message. You will see the name, the type, (.doc, .xls, .jpg etc.) and the size of the attachment.

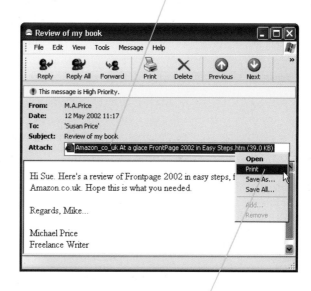

Select the attachment and right click. From the menu you can select to print it. You will not need to open the attachment to do this.

You can select to open the attachment from this menu or you can double click on the name. In either case you will be prompted with a warning.

A copy of the attachment will remain with the original e-mail in the Inbox.

4 To be able to open the attachment, the file type must be registered on your system. This means it will have an associated application. See page 19 for more detail.

5 By preference you should save the attachment to disk. This will give you an opportunity to check out the file for viruses before processing it. You will see in the Warning message that the default is to save the file this way.

6 Select OK to save the file to disk, and you will be presented with the My Documents folder. You can browse to select a different folder, and accept or modify the file name, although you must retain the file type, e.g. .htm.

7 A more direct way of saving an attachment is to select File, Save Attachments.

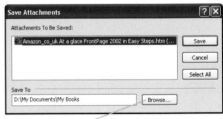

8 The Save Attachments window lists files attached to the message, and allows you to browse the folders to select where you wish to save.

9 Click OK when you have selected the folder. You will then be able to confirm the file name and save the attachment.

Create e-mail

There are two easy ways to create a new e-mail.

1 Double click the name of the addressee in the Contacts pane. This will take you to the New Message window and complete the To: box.

When you complete the Subject bar the Title bar changes from New Message to the subject. In effect, the subject becomes the file name.

2 You can click on the Create Mail button in the Toolbar. This also brings you to the New Message window. You will see that the From box has been filled in with your e-mail address. If you have more than one address, click the down arrow in the From bar and select which identity to use.

There is more information on selecting recipients later in the unit when we look at sending copies of e-mail. See page 65.

When you type in the recipient's address, you must make sure to get it absolutely correct including all symbols such as @ and underscores.

3 To complete the To: box, you can type in the address yourself, or click on the word To: which will open the Select Recipients window for you to choose a name. See page 65.

4 Complete the Subject box. If you leave this blank, you'll get a warning that there's no subject, when the message is sent.

To see the Toolbars and Status bar, select View from the menu bar and tick the bars you want.

5 You will see above the typing area the usual text formatting bar so that you can use bold, underline etc. in your message. If you select Format, Background, you can choose colour and sound! You can also choose to apply Stationery effects when you initially create the message, although not everyone can see this formatting when they receive the message.

Although you can send formatted text and stationery, it is not required by CLAIT.

6 Type in your message. The spell check facility is available, as well as the normal editing tools.

7 If you are unable to complete your e-mail message, and wish to save but not send, click File, Save. The message will be put in the Drafts folder. To open it, single click on the Drafts folder in the folder pane. The message will appear listed on the right. Double click the message, it will open and you can continue.

Send, reply and forward

1 Click the To: button (see page 63) to open the Select Recipient window. Double click the name, or select the name and click on the To: button. Do this for each main recipient; you can have several.

 This uses the address book. For more information on using and managing addresses, see page 59.

2 You can use the Cc: box to send carbon or courtesy copies to others. Select the name and click the Cc: box.

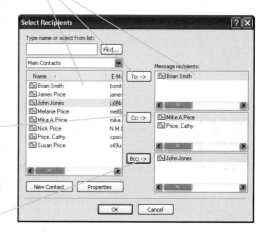

 Everyone can see the main and copied recipients. Only the sender and the receiver themselves know who gets the Bcc.

3 The Bcc: box means a blind (or hidden) carbon copy.

4 When you have completed the message you can decide whether to send now or later. To send now, select the Send button. If you are on-line the message will be sent immediately. If you are off-line, the message will be sent to the Outbox where it will remain until you next connect.

 To de-select a name in the recipient's box, just select it and press delete.

Send

5 You can decide to Send Later. This facility allows you to write all your e-mails before you connect. When you do connect, all the mail is sent at once.

 Check that a copy of the message will be put in the Sent Items folder. See the Hot Tip on page 57. At the end of the exercise, you will be required to print a copy of all the messages sent.

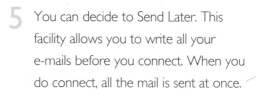

6 If you are working off-line, click Send/ Receive to connect and send.

Reply

Replying to an e-mail is probably the easiest and quickest way to communicate.

Using Reply All can cause the equivalent of a chain letter, so think carefully before you use it.

1 Select the message and click on Reply. If there were several recipients you can choose Reply All.

2 You will see that the message header has been completed for you. Re: has been inserted in the Subject box.

You can reply to a message many times.

For the CLAIT exercise, a printed copy of the Reply message will be required. It must include Re: in the Subject box.

3 The first lines of the message area start off blank for you to insert your response.

4 The original message is part of the reply, but the attachment will be dropped. When you have completed your reply, click Send.

Forward

Forwarding a message works in a similar fashion as replying to a message.

1 Select the e-mail from the Inbox list and click on the Forward button. Alternatively, from the menu you can select Message, Forward.

2 You must complete the To: box yourself. You can type in the address, or click on the To: and invoke the address book. Add Cc entries as required.

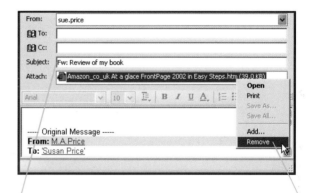

For the CLAIT exercise, a printed copy of the Forwarded message will be required. It must include Fw: in the Subject box.

3 This time the Subject box contains Fw: in front of the subject. The attachment and the original message are included.

4 You may decide that it is inappropriate to include the attachment. Select the attachment and right click. You now have the option to remove it.

5 Outlook Express modifies the e-mail icons so you can understand the status of the messages.

 Unopened   Reply

 Read   Forward

Send an attachment

1 Create your e-mail and fill in the details on the message header.

For the New CLAIT exercise, you will use the Internet to find a specific image file and save it for later use. It is this file that you will need to attach to your e-mail.

2 Select Insert Attachment or click on the Attach button. This will open the Insert Attachment window.

Attach

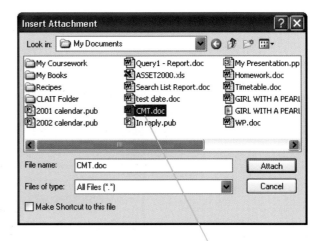

When you send an attachment, consider the size of the file. If your recipient has a slow connection, it can take a long time to download the file.

3 Browse the folders until you locate the file to attach. Notice that at this point the Files of type box is set to look for all files. With large folders, select the down arrow on the box and choose a file type to act as a filter.

4 Click the Attach button. You will return to your message, and the header section will now include an attachment with file type indicator and size.

Using Zip files is not a New CLAIT requirement.

For large files, Windows XP has a Zip compression facility.

Organise your mail

Your Inbox, like any other storage medium, needs to be monitored and organised. After you have read your e-mail, you have to decide what course of action to take.

1 To delete messages, just select them and press the delete key or click the delete button.

Messages will remain in your Deleted Items folder until you decide to empty it. Right click the folder, or select Edit, Empty Deleted Items folder.

2 You can drag and drop messages into the Deleted Items folder.

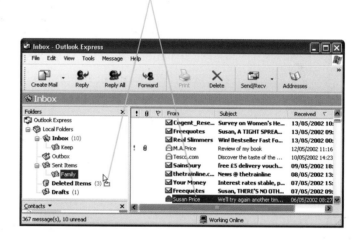

Select Tools, Options, and click the Maintenance tab to see ways to manage message storage.

3 To delete several messages at once: select the first item, then hold down Ctrl and select the others. For a block of files: select the first item, then hold down the Shift and click on the last. Press delete.

You cannot drag and drop items into the Outbox. You will get a No Entry symbol as you pass over the folder.

4 The messages arrive and are stored in date order. Click Received in the heading to reverse the order and view the oldest messages. Click From to view them grouped by sender.

5 You can create your own folders to organise your e-mail. Select the main folder, right click and select New Folder from the menu. Name the folder, then drag and drop messages into it.

Print your e-mail

New CLAIT requires you to provide printed copies of all the e-mail you have sent and received. It is usually the last step in the exercise. Make sure that Outlook Express is set up to save a copy of all e-mail in the Sent folder.

You can print a message without opening it. Select it from the folder and click the Print button.

To print messages in the Inbox or the Sent folder:

1 Open the message. Then select File, Print, or click the printer button.

When you create and print a new e-mail, you must not have Re: or Fw: in the subject heading, i.e. it must be new.

2 The Print dialog box opens, and allows you to select a page range, and number of copies. If you have more than one printer defined you can also select the printer. Click Print to action the request.

To print the attachment, save it to disk, and use the appropriate software to view and print it. You can also print it using the method described on page 61.

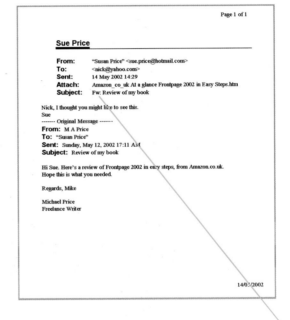

Outlook Express should automatically include all the required details in the header, but do check the printout to make sure.

3 The printed e-mail for a reply or forward must show Re: or Fw: and the original subject heading. The address on a reply must be the same as that on the original message. If the message had an attachment, that also must show in the heading.

The World Wide Web

Internet Explorer is the Web browser supplied by Microsoft. It can be started from the Start menu, or from the Quick Launch bar.

The Home Page

The first screen that you will see is known as the Home page. As Internet Explorer is a Microsoft

product, the standard is to open with the Microsoft Home page. You will see the MSN address in the address bar. The page presents you with information, news, advertisements etc., and a series of links to other pages.

Notice also the scroll bars at the side of the page. The full Home page is not displayed.

Internet Explorer Toolbar   Hotmail e-mail   Chat rooms   Search

Status bar displaying address of selected link   news   links to topics

You can navigate the Internet by typing any address into the address bar. Then click on Go. This is sometimes the most efficient way to use the Internet. Click the down arrow on the Address bar to select sites previously visited. Alternatively, you can use the hypertext links that are found on most pages. Use the toolbar with its Back, Forward etc. buttons for navigating whilst you are surfing.

The Links

A link, or more correctly a hypertext link, is a pointer to the address of either another part of the same page, another page on the same site or another site altogether. To recognise a link, pass the mouse pointer over the screen. It changes to a hand when on a link. A link may also be indicated by underlined text. A link on a Web page is created by using a Uniform Resource Locator (URL).

If the new page has many images, it may take a long time to load. Watch the progression on the status bar to make sure it is still loading the information.

The URL

This is the address of a Web site. It takes the following form:

$$\text{http://www.msn.co.uk/default.asp}$$

access mechanism   server   page

Click on the link and you will be taken to that address. The status bar shows the page opening and the progress.

There are two meanings of Home page. One you select for your Home page when you open Internet Explorer, the other is a site Home page. When you click the Home button you return to your starting Home page.

The Internet Explorer Toolbar

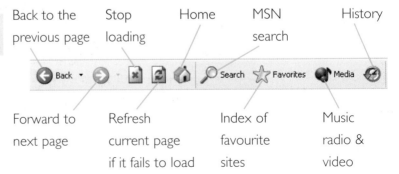

Back to the previous page

Stop loading

Home

MSN search

History

Forward to next page

Refresh current page if it fails to load

Index of favourite sites

Music radio & video

Use Stop (loading) if you change your mind after selecting a link.

Search engines

Using a search engine when surfing the Internet can save time and frustration, but you must first get to know which type of engine will best return the result you want, and that may differ from search to search.

This is a directory search that finds Web sites associated with your topic. Use this when you want general information about the subject.

Web Site Searches

MSN (http://search.msn.co.uk) for example will perform a search to find Web sites that match your general category. It provides domain results i.e. site addresses that match the topic and divides the sites into Sponsored and Directory sites.

1 Select Search from the MSN home page. You may wish to limit your search to the UK.

The down arrow next to the Back button will let you select which page you wish to return to.

2 Type in the search topic and click on Search.

Searching on 'Roses' with MSN Search returned 277 results.

3 Check the shortcuts to categories of results. This may speed up finding the sites you really want.

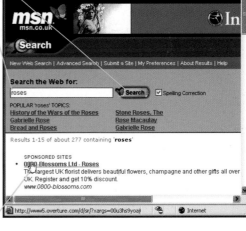

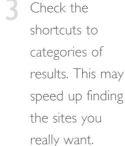

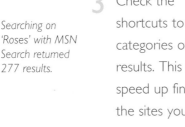

To return to the Search results page, select the Back button.

4 Scroll through the pages. When you find a site to investigate, select it. You will be taken to the site Home page.

5 If there are many pages of results, try the Advanced search, or add more words to refine the search.

Web Page Searches

Use this type of search when you want a specific piece of information about the topic.

Some search engines, e.g. Google (http://www.google.com) examine individual pages within the Web sites, to identify those that have the text specified in your search criteria. When you click on a link, you will be transferred to a page within a site.

Searching on 'Roses' with Google returned 2.5 million results.

1 The results from a Web page search returns so many hits, that it becomes essential to learn some of the more advanced tricks and techniques to refine your search.

For New CLAIT you must provide a printout with the required information, not just a search engine list of sites.

2 Most search engines provide useful tips, and forms for you to complete, to help limit the number of hits.

Combination Searches

Yahoo.com (http://search.yahoo.com) will sort the information. You can decide on your level of interest and go straight there.

Some search engines will search both sites and pages and categorise the result for you.

General   Specific   Up-to-date   In depth

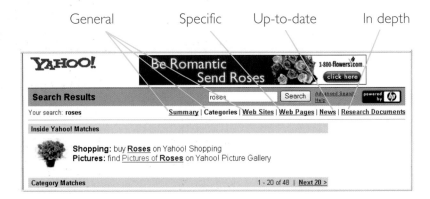

Local Search engines

A good Web site will also have links to Other Web sites of similar content or interest.

Most Web sites consist of several Web pages. They will have their own Home page, navigation facility and often a search engine as well. The search engine works within the site, and all resulting links will be to pages within the site.

This site offers its own navigation facility. Click on the down arrow to choose which section of the site to visit.

1 With The National Trust Gardens site, the search facility is on the main Home page. Type in the topic of interest, and select search.

2 The results will be restricted to the National Trust and its gardens.

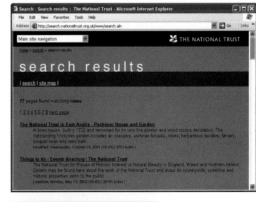

3 You will also find an advanced search facility to generate a more specific list.

Save images and text

This toolbar will only appear if the image size is 200x200 pixels or more, and if you have Internet Explorer v6 or later.

Save the image

e-mail

Image toolbar

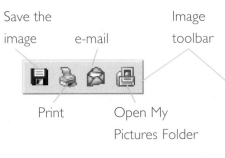

Print

Open My Pictures Folder

To save an image to your hard disk for later use:

1 Find and select the image.

2 Click the Save the image button, or right click the image. From the menu select Save Picture As.

For New CLAIT you must find the required image and save it to your hard disk so that you can then attach it to an e-mail. It is not sufficient to use the menu option to e-mail the picture.

3 This will open the My Pictures folder. You can save the picture there, or navigate to another folder.

4 Note that the image is saved in the JPEG or .jpg format. These are the standard formats for Internet photographs and picture files as they use high compression.

.gif files are used for icons and small images.

5 Click on Save and make a note of the file name for later reference.

Web pages can be constructed in different ways and a neat A4 printout is not guaranteed. It is therefore unlikely that you will get asked in New CLAIT to save text from the Internet.

You can learn more about Web page construction in Unit 9. See page 190.

If you just want to save and view items from a Web page, Word is a good application to use. It works well with a combination of text and graphics and is also able to create and work with .htm and .html files – the format for Web pages.

You must be very careful not to infringe copyright. If in any doubt, contact the Web Master for the site.

The method you use to save text from a Web page will depend on how much text you wish to copy, and your purpose in copying.

1. For a small amount of text, to be used in a Word or text application, use the normal copy and paste facility. Select the text with the mouse or cursor, right click and copy, open Word or another application and paste. The pasted text is normal unformatted text.

2. For the whole contents of the Web page, text and images, you can use Edit, Select all or Ctrl+A and copy. Open Word and select paste. The pasted items may carry certain attributes with them, and the result in Word may be different than you'd expect. The objects may be encased in frames or need to be realigned on the page. You then have the choice to save the document as a standard .doc file, or as an .htm or .html.

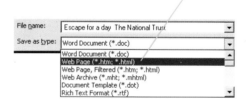

3. Unlike Word, Internet Explorer is specifically designed to work with Web pages, and offers to Edit with Microsoft FrontPage. Using this, you could capture objects from Web pages and use them for your own purposes. When you save the file, .htm and .html are the default, or you can choose a text file.

Manage Web addresses

The History button lists Web sites visited over a period of time. You can use Web addresses from the list. Open and close History as for Favorites.

Internet Explorer provides the Favorites function to allow you to store Web addresses that you wish to use again.

1 Make sure that you are viewing the page that you wish to bookmark or add to your favorites list. Select Favorites from the menu.

You can also right click a Web page and select Add to Favorites from there.

2 Click Add to Favorites. The Add Favorite dialog box picks up the title of the site and its Internet address. To help with the organisation, it allows you to collect related links together in folders of favorites.

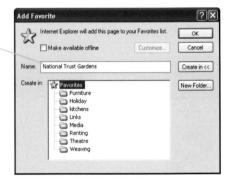

You don't have to organise your Favorites into folders, but over a period of time it makes sense.

3 To use an existing folder, select "Create in" and the list of folders expands for you to select. For a new topic, select New Folder. Type in the folder name and then click OK.

Both the Favorites and History buttons are toggles – click once to open, click again to close.

4 To view the list of Favorites, select the Favorites button on the toolbar. The list of your bookmarked or saved addresses will appear in a separate pane on the left side of the screen. Click a folder to open it and select from the list. Close the folder (X) to return to the full Web page screen.

Printing Web pages

Web pages do not necessarily conform to screen or paper dimensions and screen and printer resolutions also differ. Much of the time you can only see a portion of the Web page, the scroll bars allow you see the rest. It is always worth previewing the printed output first to ascertain just how many pages you will take, and whether it will look the way you expect.

1 With your required Web page on the screen, select File, Print Preview. The toolbar shows Page 1 of 1, and the magnification.

Select Setup and change the paper size to A4 if necessary.

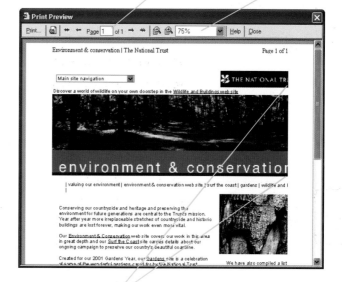

You will not be penalised if the text does truncate, as long as the page has the required information.

2 Notice how the titles have been truncated on the right. Also, the original text background was green, but is rendered as white when printed.

You can print a table of links, useful if you are doing research and need to keep track of sites visited.

3 Some Web pages are composed of 'frames' which can be printed together, as on the screen, or individually.

Exercise

You are allowed two hours to complete this assignment.

See page 233 Step 2 for information on how to receive an initial e-mail message with an attachment. The message will come from the Heronsbrook manager at HGC@prient.co.uk

Scenario

You work as a research assistant at Surprise Gardens. The Manager at Heronsbrook Garden Centre has sent you an e-mail message.

1. Open your mailbox and read the message entitled Pan Statue.

    Add the sender's e-mail address to your address book. Print a copy of the attached file, Pan.jpg

Your supervisor is interested in buying the statue.

2. Prepare to forward the message Pan Statue and its attachment to your supervisor at SGC@prient.co.uk, adding the following text:

    Further to your enquiry, I am forwarding information I have received about the statue of Pan.

    Add your name and exam centre number to the end of your message.

    Check your message for errors and forward the e-mail message including the attachment. Make sure that your system keeps a copy of the outgoing message.

You should acknowledge receipt of the original e-mail.

3. Prepare a reply to the Heronsbrook Manager with the following message:

    Thank you for the information about the Pan statue. I will contact you again once my supervisor has made a decision.

    Add your name and exam centre number to the end of your message.

    Check your message for errors and forward the e-mail message. Make sure that your system keeps a copy of the outgoing message.

You need to manage your mailbox to reduce storage demands.

4. Save the attachment Pan.gif separately from the mailbox and delete the message Pan Statue.

Your supervisor will give a talk on National Trust Gardens, and has asked you to find some facts and figures for his talk.

5.   Use a Web-based search engine to search for Web pages that contain information about National Trust Gardens. Follow links to find specific facts and figures on this subject. Bookmark the page and print one copy.

Your supervisor has suggested that you might find it helpful in your work if you had some computer reference books to hand.

6.   Access the Amazon Web site at www.amazon.co.uk Click the Books link and use the local search facility to find books on FrontPage. Bookmark the page and print one copy. Save the cover of a book as Frontpage.jpg.

Prepare an e-mail to send to your supervisor.

7.   Give the message the subject heading: Reference Books
Use the following message:
Here is the front cover of one of the reference books I would find very useful. Please let me know if I am able to order it.

Locate and attach the file Frontpage.jpg.
Add your name and exam centre number to the end of your message.

Send a copy of the message to the Heronsbrook Manager.

Check your message for errors and forward the e-mail message including the attachment. Make sure that your system keeps a copy of the outgoing message.

8.   Locate copies of the messages you have sent and print a copy of each message. Make sure header details (To, From, Date, Subject) are shown. Make sure attachment details are shown where appropriate.

9.   Access the bookmark facility and make sure that you have stored the URLs.

10.   Exit the software correctly.

Checklist

When you have finished the exercise, use the following checklist. Have you:

- Created and saved the required e-mail with the correct address
- Opened, replied and forwarded the required e-mail with attachments where necessary
- Sent a copy of the required e-mail using the cc facility
- Stored, recalled and printed the attachment
- Accessed the specified Web page
- Searched for and located required information
- Stored URLs and e-mail addresses for later recall
- Printed copies of the messages you have sent

Answers

FrontPage.jpg

Pan.jpg

Spreadsheets

This unit covers using the Excel spreadsheet to enter, edit and present numerical data. It includes using and copying formulae, saving and printing.

Covers

Unit Four

The spreadsheet

To start Excel, select Start, All Programs, Microsoft Excel.

In Unit 7 you will learn how to use Excel to create graphs and charts. It can also be used as a database program.

The spreadsheet design is based on the ledger sheet. Information is entered in columns and rows, with each cell (the intersection of a column and a row) containing one item of data. Each cell has a cell reference or address, A1, B6, etc. The spreadsheet has columns from A-Z, AA-AZ, BA-BZ and so on and 65,000 rows. The spreadsheet window has both familiar features and new ones.

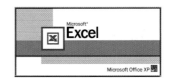

1. The window has the usual Title Bar, Menu bar and Toolbar, with the Standard and Formatting bars sharing one row. We can also see the Task Pane, with its various options.

To put Standard and Formatting bars on separate rows to see more buttons, click on

2. The Formula bar showing the cursor position as a cell reference, in this case A1. It will also show the data contents of the cell.

The current cell (and typing location/cursor) is the black rectangle.

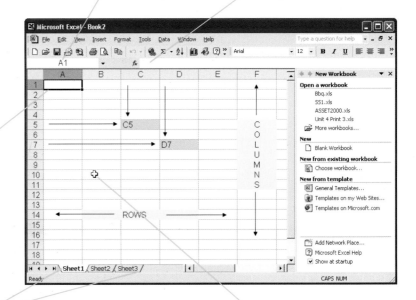

The spreadsheet is known as a Workbook, it normally has three sheets, but you can add more. To move to another sheet, just click on the tab.

3. The mouse takes the shape of a large + which floats over the spreadsheet grid. You must click on a cell to make it the active or current cell, as referenced in the formula bar.

A cell address always begins with a letter, e.g. C5.

Work in the spreadsheet is based on the cell. You enter data into cells and use their cell address as a reference. Later in the unit, you will learn how to use the cell address in formulae.

A series of consecutive cells is known as a range. A range can consist of part of a row or column or a combination of both.

To select a range, press the left mouse button and drag to cover the required cells.

Cell references can be typed in upper or lower case.

4 The range identified in green is B4:D4. The colon in the range reference means include all the cells in between.

You can name a range of cells and use it as a reference point to go to in the spreadsheet, or use it in formula. This is not a New CLAIT Level 1 requirement.

5 The range identified in blue is B6:D8. This range has been selected using the cursor. The white cell, B6, is the starting point of the selection. The first cell in any selection will always remain white.

To Unfreeze panes, just select Window, Unfreeze Panes from any location on the sheet.

6 When you are working with a larger spreadsheet than will fit the screen, as you scroll further down or to the right, you will lose sight of your row or column labels. To fix them so they remain visible, position the cursor below and to the right of the labels, B4 in the sample shown above, and select Window, Freeze Panes.

Create a spreadsheet

For the New CLAIT course you will only need to create a small spreadsheet, with very simple formulae. To enter data:

1 Type the spreadsheet title in cell A1. You must press Enter for it to be inserted. The cursor moves automatically down one cell. For this reason, you may find it easier to enter the data in columns.

2 You should normally enter the data into consecutive cells, without leaving any empty columns or rows, although a blank row under the title is acceptable.

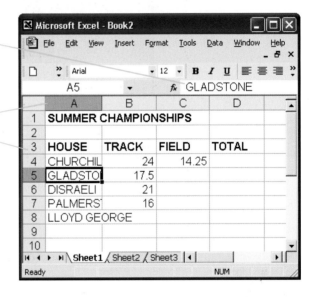

3 As you enter data into the cells, you will see that text is always left aligned, and numbers right aligned. Decimals are displayed as typed.

4 To amend an entry, you can just retype it. You can also double click a cell or press F2, both of which will position the cursor within the cell for you to make changes.

Change the layout

You will need to make changes to the spreadsheet layout.

When you widen a column, it is widened all the way down the spreadsheet.

1. The columns are not wide enough to display the full cell contents. Where the adjoining cell to the right remains empty, the full text is displayed. Where there is data in the adjoining cell, the full contents remain, but the display is truncated.

2. To widen the column, first click on the widest entry, then select Format, Column, AutoFit Selection.

Make sure that the column is wide enough even when printed. If you add or amend an entry, don't forget to check the column width again.

If your column is not wide enough to display all the numeric data, you will see a series of hash signs. Just widen the column to view the data.

TOTAL
######
######
######
######
######

3. You can also widen the column by positioning the mouse over the divider on the column heading. When you get the double-headed arrow, double click, or press the left mouse button and drag to the width you require. Notice, however, that the title is the widest entry in column A and double clicking would widen the column to accommodate it, not the row label entries.

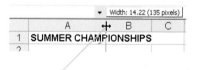

Another required change to the layout is to insert or delete columns and rows.

If you insert the new row or column in the wrong place, just click Undo.

If you highlight or select more than one column or row, the number you have chosen will be inserted. See the Hot Tip on page 85 for selecting cells.

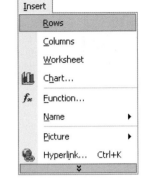

1 Columns are inserted to the left of the cursor, and rows above. When you have positioned the cursor, select Insert, and pick columns or rows as appropriate.

2 The inserted column or row will have a Smart Tag attached to it. This facility allows you to apply a format to the column. Click on the Smart Tag to display the Format menu.

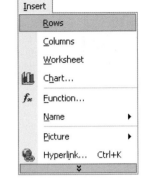

Alignment of the column titles is important in New CLAIT. See page 99 for more information.

3 If you copy the format (from the left or the right column) when you insert a column, your column titles should maintain the alignment you have already chosen.

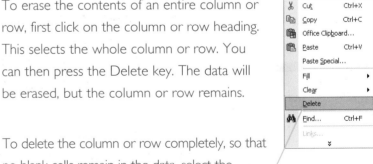

4 To erase the contents of an entire column or row, first click on the column or row heading. This selects the whole column or row. You can then press the Delete key. The data will be erased, but the column or row remains.

Excel offers the facility to hide columns and rows. However, this only hides the data, the values will still be included in any formulae. When you are instructed to delete a column or row, you must remove it completely.

5 To delete the column or row completely, so that no blank cells remain in the data, select the column or row, as above, and click on Edit and Delete. The row or column disappears, and the adjacent ones slide along to fill the gap.

Once you have typed data into the spreadsheet, you should seldom need to retype it. As well as inserting and deleting columns and rows, you can move the contents of cells.

When you delete a column or row, it affects the whole of the spreadsheet. Make sure that any data that is not currently visible is also not required.

1 If you select Edit, Delete without selecting a whole column or row, you will be offered the option to move cells. Use this option if you have misaligned your data or want to delete a section of a row, not across the whole width of the spreadsheet.

2 You can move the contents of cells quickly and easily with the mouse pointer. Select a cell or range of cells and position the mouse on any edge of the range. A four-headed arrow appears, and you can then drag and drop to the required position. Any existing data will be over-written.

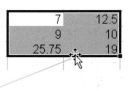

When you insert or delete columns or rows, or if you move cells, Excel automatically adjusts any formulae that reference the range involved. See page 97 for more details on recalculating formulae.

You can also use Cut and Paste to move cells:

3 Select the cells you wish to move. Stay on the selected cells and click with the right mouse button. From the menu, select the entry Cut. The selected cells will be outlined by a flashing box and will remain on the screen.

Save your spreadsheet when required. See Unit 1, Using a Computer, page 22.

4 Click on the target cell and select the Paste entry. Pasted cells retain their relative positions.

5 To remove the flashing outline, press Escape on the keyboard.

Creating formulae

The spreadsheet formulae work with standard mathematical notation and with cell references. All formulae start with = (an equals sign), this is the indicator to the application that this cell contains a formula.

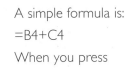

Position the cursor where you want the formula.

I A simple formula is:

=B4+C4

When you press Enter, Excel calculates the answer and shows it in the active cell. The Formula bar displays the actual formula. If you change the contents of the referenced cells, the result is recalculated.

If you are unfamiliar with using brackets in arithmetic, consider the following:
2+2*4=10 (multipy first)
(2+2)*4=16 (brackets first)

2 You can use any operators, + (plus) - (minus) * (multipy) / (divide), and you can use them in combination. The normal rules of mathematical precedence apply, i.e. brackets are calculated first, then multiplication and division, and finally addition and subtraction.

Once you have typed an = sign, Excel will let you move the mouse or cursor to select any cell. When you click on a cell you will see the cell reference appear in the formula box.

3 It is possible to type the cell references in the formula, but often easier and more accurate to select them with the mouse. First position the cursor in the correct cell, in the example D4. Type an = sign. Click with the mouse on the first cell, B4, type the + sign, and click with the mouse on the second cell, C4. Press Enter, or click on the tick.

When you are constructing a formula, only click on cells that you wish to include.
Check your cell references and formulae before you press Enter.

4 If you prefer to use the keyboard, type = and move the cursor to B4, type the + and move to C4. Then press Enter.

Functions

A function carries out a mathematical or statistical calculation.

The example formula shown on the previous page is very simple and straightforward. Most of the formulae you will be required to create in the New CLAIT course will be just as easy, multiplying one cell by another, or dividing one by another etc. You should try to use simple formulae whenever possible.

Excel allows you to use pre-defined functions in the spreadsheet, and it lets you work with ranges of cells in calculations, rather than identifying cell addresses individually. To help you select and use the function you need, Excel provides a Function Wizard.

To view the list of Functions, select the Insert Function button on the Formula bar.

1 The list is divided into categories to make it easier to find an appropriate formula.

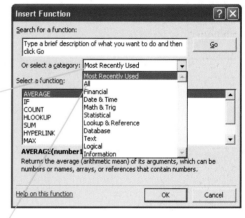

2 Currently showing are the Most Recently Used. To see all possible functions, select All from the list.

3 If you are not sure of which function is appropriate, you can type a description of your requirement and click Go.

4 The Wizard suggests some possibilities and as you select each one, provides a brief description of how it works below.

Press Esc on the keyboard, if you start the AutoSum function and realise your cursor is in the wrong cell. Any previous cell contents will be restored.

The AutoSum function is the most commonly used. It adds together columns or rows of figures. You can type it yourself, as with any formula, or you can use the AutoSum function on the toolbar. The Sum function syntax is =SUM(cell reference:cell reference). The (cell reference:cell reference) represents a range of cells, for example B4 to B8. To use AutoSum:

On page 90 we added the contents of just two cells – using the Sum function we can add whole columns or rows of figures quickly and easily.

1 Position the cursor in the cell where you wish to place the total or answer. Click the AutoSum button.

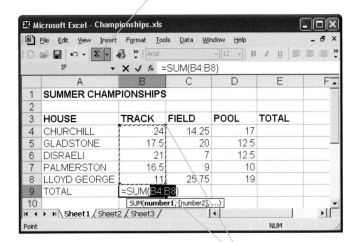

2 The AutoSum function will create the formula to total the column of figures above the cursor. You will see the suggested range outlined. Check that it has selected the correct range of cells, and press Enter, or click the tick.

3 The AutoSum function will not include a cell containing text, or an empty cell. It only selects the range up to that point. However, you can re-select the range of cells with the mouse. While the range of cells in the formula is still highlighted (yellow on black), click on the first cell and drag to select the correct range. You will see the cell reference in the brackets change. When it is correct, press Enter.

4 The AutoSum function adds the contents in a row in a similar way. Position the cursor at the end of the row of figures and click the AutoSum button. The figures to the left will be totalled. This only works this way for the first two rows in a column of values.

You must check which cell range AutoSum has selected. It doesn't always get it right.

3	HOUSE	TRACK	FIELD	POOL	TOTAL	
4	CHURCHILL	24	14.25	17	55.25	
5	GLADSTONE	17.5	20	12.5	=SUM(B5:D5)	
6	DISRAELI	21	7	12.5	SUM(**number1**, [number2], …)	

5 When there are no figures, or only one figure, above the cursor, AutoSum will automatically add the row.

You will only use AutoSum for the first row in the spreadsheet. For the rest of the rows you MUST use the Fill by Example feature. See page 96 on copying formulae.

3	HOUSE	TRACK	FIELD	POOL	TOTAL	
4	CHURCHILL	24	14.25	17	55.25	
5	GLADSTONE	17.5	20	12.5	50	
6	DISRAELI	21	7	12.5	=SUM(E4:E5)	
7	PALMERSTON	16.5	9	10	SUM(**number1**, [number2], …)	

6 If there are two or more figures above the cursor, AutoSum will automatically add column-wise.

The Average function is similar in format to Sum: =Average(cell address:cell address). To use the Average function:

1 Click on the down arrow next to the AutoSum and select Average.

2 Check the range it has selected. In this example, the default selection would give an incorrect result, so you must adjust it.

You don't want the Total value included in the Average calculation.

3	HOUSE	TRACK	FIELD	POOL	TOTAL	AVERAGE	
4	CHURCHILL	24	14.25	17	55.25	=AVERAGE(B4:E4)	
5	GLADSTONE	17.5	20	12.5		AVERAGE(**number1**, [number2], …)	

Many of the functions are complex and require the user to have a mathematical background. Some, like Max, Min and Average are much easier to use and it is a good idea to use one of these to familiarise yourself with how the Insert Function works.

The Function Arguments dialog box attempts to explain the formula. Sometimes its use of jargon is self-defeating.

The Arguments are simply the range of cells you wish to use in the formula. You can select a second range of cells to include in the formula if required.

You must check which cell range the function has selected. It doesn't always get it right.

The Collapse dialog feature is used in other Excel areas such as creating charts.

1 Position the cursor where you want your Average formula. Select Insert Function, choose Average and click OK.

2 The Function Arguments dialog box appears. The black box is the range of cells that it is using in its formula. It shows the actual data selected and the result of the formula. It is always wise to confirm the range it has chosen, so click the Collapse Dialog button.

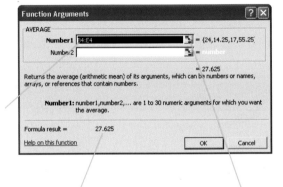

3 The Function Arguments window remains, but only the selection box is available. As in the previous Average formula, the Total cell is wrongly included, so use the mouse to re-select the range.

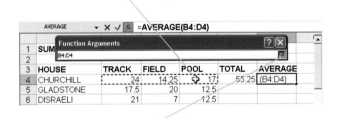

4 Click again on the button to expand the dialog box and return to the Function Argument window. When finished click on OK and you will return to the spreadsheet.

The Fill tool

Excel provides the Fill tool to enable swift data entry of standard items such as days and months, dates, numbers and series of any type. It even allows you to create your own lists, for use with the Fill tool.

1 The Fill option is found in the Edit menu, but is more easily accessed by positioning the mouse on the bottom right corner of the active cell. You will see the mouse symbol change to a black +.

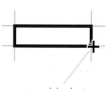

2 To fill a range of cells, select the starting cell and position the mouse on the Fill handle. Press the left mouse button and drag in the direction you wish to fill.

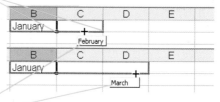

When you fill with months you can start with any month. When you fill with days you can start with any day, and the Fill options offer to fill with just weekdays.

3 As you drag you will get an indication of the fill data. Release the mouse to complete the fill.

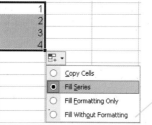

4 You can fill a range with an incremental series. First create and select the pattern, in these examples you will need to select two cells. Use the Fill handle at the bottom of the selection and drag and release as before.

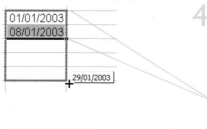

The first option to Copy Cells would have filled the range with just the number one.

5 When you have filled the range, you will see a smart tag with a range of fill options.

Copying formulae

The spreadsheet works with cell references, which could be a single cell, or a range of cells. In formulae these references are described as relative or absolute.

A relative reference is based on the relative position of cells. So a formula that totals a column is adding the cells above it. A formula that totals a row to the left, is adding the cells to the left of it. The relative reference is the norm.

You are not required to use absolute cell references in New CLAIT.

An absolute reference refers always to a specific cell. To make a reference absolute you must include $ (the dollar sign) as part of the cell reference, for example F7.

When you copy relative formulae the cell references automatically adjust. When you copy formulae that contain absolute references, those cell references remain the same.

To copy formula:

1 Select your first formula, whether in the first column or row.

You are required to replicate or copy formulae in CLAIT. The easiest way to do this is with the Fill facility. You could also use copy and paste.

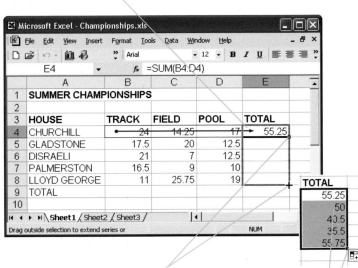

2 Use the Fill handle to drag down or across the range of cells, and release. A formula based on the relative position will be copied to each cell and the result calculated.

Recalculate

If you insert a column or row, the insertion point will affect whether or not its data is included. In the example illustrated on the previous page, the formula in E4 references the range B4:D4.

When you change numeric data in the spreadsheet, formulae that reference those cells will recalculate the result. This also happens when you delete columns and rows.

1 If you insert a new column between B and D, the data will be included automatically in the calculation.

This is a new feature in Excel 2002 (the Office XP version).

2 If you insert a new column between D and E, outside the current range but before the formula, the data will still automatically be included in the calculation. Excel indicates this by moving the cursor to the formula cell.

Always check your formulae to make sure they are correct.

3 If you insert a new column between A and B, this cell is not referenced in the formula and there is no recalculation. However, a small indicator appears top left in the formula cell.

TOTAL
55.25

Notice how Excel has adjusted the formula already to recognise the insertion of a column: B4:D4 has become C4:E4.

Microsoft Excel - Championships.xls

File Edit View Insert Format Tools Data Window Help

Arial ▾ 12 ▾ **B** *I* U ≡ ≡ ≡

F4 *fx* =SUM(C4:E4)

	A	B	C	D	E	F
1	SUMMER CHAMPIONSHIPS					
2						
3	HOUSE	FUN GAMES	TRACK	FIELD	POOL	TOTAL
4	CHURCHILL	10	24	14.25	◇7	55.25
5	GLADSTONE		17.5	20	12.5	50
6	DISRAELI		21	7	12.5	40.5
7	PALMERSTON		16.5	9	10	35.5
8	LLOYD GEORGE		11	25.75	19	55.75
9	TOTAL					

Sheet1 / Sheet2 / Sheet3 /

Ready CAPS NUM

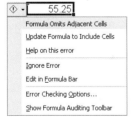

◇ ▾ 55.25

Formula Omits Adjacent Cells
Update Formula to Include Cells
Help on this error
Ignore Error
Edit in Formula Bar
Error Checking Options...
Show Formula Auditing Toolbar

4 When you click on the formula cell, a warning exclamation appears, indicating that the data in the new column has not been included.

Numeric format

Integer simply means whole numbers with no decimal places.

At some point during the CLAIT exercise, you will be required to present numbers to a required number of decimal places, and/or with a currency symbol.

To format numbers:

Although numbers may be displayed in integer format, calculations will still be performed using the exact number, including decimal values.

1 Select the range of cells to format. Remember that the first cell in any selection remains white.

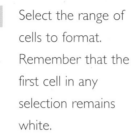

When you format the column to currency you will need to widen it or you'll only see hash signs. See page 87.

2 Select Format Cells from the menu, and from the Category list click on Number. You can now choose the number of decimal places, to use commas in thousands, and how to display negative numbers.

The Currency button on the toolbar is not a toggle switch. If you decide not to use currency format, reselect the cells and choose Format, Cells, General or Number.

3 Select Currency or Accounting to display the £ sign in each cell. The Accounting format aligns the £ symbol to the left of the cell. You can also select the Euro symbol if you wish.

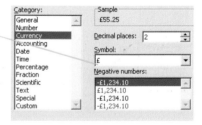

When using the Increase and Decrease Decimal buttons, you will need to increase decimals until all your numbers display the same, then decrease until you have the required number.

4 The Formatting toolbar provides easy access to some formats.

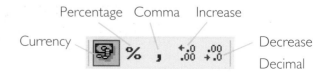

Currency Percentage Comma Increase Decrease Decimal

Text format

Check your heading alignment after you have inserted a new column to ensure that you meet the requirements.

The only text formatting you are required to use in the spreadsheet unit is to right align the specified titles, usually those over numbers. Text alignment and formatting works with the same buttons as in word processing. Select the headings and click on the Align Right button.

Align Right

You can, however, experiment with the alignment options to enhance the spreadsheet for your own purposes.

1 Select the cell range first, then choose Format, Cells, from the menu and select the Alignment tab.

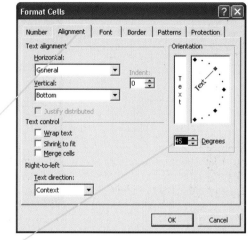

2 You will see a variety of Text alignment options, including one to change the orientation of the text. These text headings are set at 45 degrees.

This is fun to do, but it's not recommended for New CLAIT exercises.

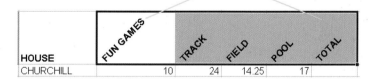

HOUSE	FUN GAMES	TRACK	FIELD	POOL	TOTAL
CHURCHILL	10	24	14.25	17	

File management is the same throughout Microsoft Office, so the methods used to Open, Close, Save, and Save As are the same for Excel as Word. See pages 29-49.

3 You can use the Text wrap button to double stack column titles.

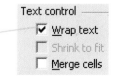

HOUSE	FUN GAMES	TRACK EVENTS	FIELD EVENTS	POOL	TOTAL
CHURCHILL	10	24	14.25	17	65.25

Printing spreadsheets

You should always use the Print Preview facility with spreadsheets. It can save time, paper and frustration.

To print the spreadsheet:

Click on File, Print Preview, or select the Print Preview button. The Preview window has its own toolbar. The Previous and Next buttons allow you to scroll through the pages. The Zoom or magnifying glass switch between full page or detail view.

Use the Close button on the toolbar to return to the spreadsheet.

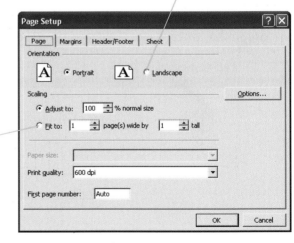

Most spreadsheet printouts require landscape orientation.

2 The Status bar indicates that the print will take two pages. To change the paper orientation, which may reduce the printout to just one page, select the Setup button and choose Landscape. Click on OK to return to the Preview window to view the result.

Only use the Fit to: option to achieve a slight reduction in size. Often it is better to print on two pages. You must be able to see all the data, so check the widest column on your finished printout to make sure.

3 If necessary, select Fit to: and reduce the print to one page.

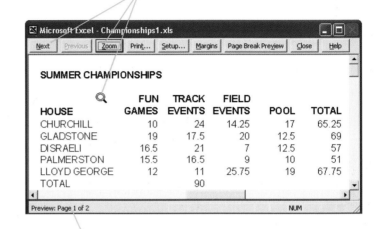

Print Formulae

It is essential to provide a printout of formulae used in the spreadsheet. Normally, formulae is only visible in the Formula bar, and the result of the calculation is shown in the cells. To view formulae used in the spreadsheet:

Use the easy shortcut to view formulae: hold down the Ctrl key and press ¬ (the key above the Tab key). This toggles you in and out of formulae view.

1 Select Tools, Options, and the View tab.

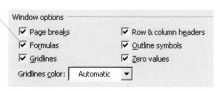

2 Tick the box for Formulas and click OK.

OCR use the term formulae, Microsoft use the more mundane formulas.

3 When you return to the spreadsheet view you will see the formulae in the spreadsheet cells. In this

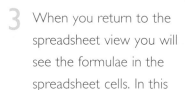

view the alignment and formatting of numbers have been dropped. You do not need to worry about this. OCR simply need to see that formulae have been used, and copied correctly.

You must check the column widths and ensure that all formulae are displayed in full, including trailing brackets – this doesn't always happen automatically. You don't need to make any other changes.

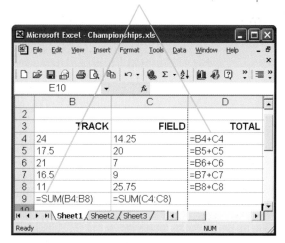

You can select an area of the spreadsheet, and in the Print dialog box choose to print Selection.

4 Select Print Preview and check the printout as before. Click the Print button to invoke the Print dialog box and select OK.

Exercise

Scenario

You are working as an administrative assistant for Surprise Garden Centres. You have been asked to produce a report showing the sales for the garden centres for the month of May.

1. Create a new spreadsheet.
2. Enter the following data.

SURPRISE GARDEN CENTRES – May 2002						
GARDEN CENTRE	PLANTS	HARDWARE	CATERING	SALES	AREA	SALES PER HECTARE
ENGLEMERE	4122	4560	1255		1.75	
HARLEQUIN	3625	3852	845		1.5	
HERONSBROOK	3745	3850	1360		2.35	
AVON	5124	5577	1295		2.33	
SILVER BROOK	3145	3321	750		3	
ROOKERY	1546	1687	426		1.9	
THE ELMS	10250	12595	2010		5	
OVERALL TOTAL						

3. Enter your name, exam centre number and today's date a few rows below the data.

4. SALES is calculated by adding together the figures for PLANTS, HARDWARE and CATERING.

   Insert a formula to calculate the SALES for ENGLEMERE.

   Replicate this formula to show the SALES for all the other garden centres.

   The OVERALL TOTAL is calculated by adding all the sales figures. Insert a formula at the bottom of the SALES column to calculate the OVERALL TOTAL.

5. The SALES PER HECTARE is calculated by dividing SALES by AREA. Insert a formula to calculate the SALES PER HECTARE for ENGLEMERE. Replicate this formula for the other centres.

6. Save your spreadsheet with the filename SALES and print one copy showing the figures, not the formulae. Make sure that all the data is displayed in full.

Your manager wants you to make some changes to the report.

7. THE ROOKERY is to be sold. Delete this entire row.

8. Make the following amendments to the spreadsheet:

The HARDWARE figure for AVON should be 4250.
The CATERING figure for SILVERBROOK should be 850.
SILVER BROOK should be spelt SILVERBROOK.

Make sure that the SALES and SALES PER HECTARE figures have updated as a result of these changes.

Your manager wants you to format the report.

9. Apply alignment as follows:

The column heading GARDEN CENTRES and all the row labels should be left aligned.
The other column headings (e.g. PLANTS) should be right aligned. All numeric data should be right aligned.

10. Format the data.

The figures for PLANTS, HARDWARE and CATERING should be in integer format (zero decimal places).
The figures for SALES, and AREA should be displayed to two decimal places.
The SALES PER HECTARE data only should be displayed with a £ sign and two decimal places.

It has been decided to include the figures for the Outbuildings franchise.

11. Insert a column headed OUTBUILDINGS between HARDWARE and CATERING.
The heading should be right aligned. The figures should be right aligned and displayed in Integer format (zero decimal places.)

Starting with ENGLEMERE and ending with THE ELMS the figures are:

ENGLEMERE	9910,	HARLEQUIN	4555,
HERONSBROOK	6858,	AVON	10150,
SILVERBROOK	7700,	THE ELMS	15800

Make sure that the figures for SALES and SALES PER HECTARE are updated to include OUTBUILDINGS.

12. Save your spreadsheet with the filename MAY SALES. Print a copy showing figures, not formulae. Make sure that all data is displayed in full.

13. Print the spreadsheet with the formulae showing. Make sure that all formulae are displayed in full.

14. Close the spreadsheet and exit the software correctly.

Checklist

When you have finished the exercise, use the following checklist. Have you:

- Created and saved the spreadsheet
- Inserted and deleted columns and rows and amended data
- Created and replicated correct formulae
- Formatted the text with the required alignment and numeric data to the correct number of decimal places
- Printed the spreadsheet with all the data showing in full

These results show the final three columns of the spreadsheet prints, so you can check your calculations.

Answers

Initial data

SALES	AREA	SALES PER HECTARE
9937	1.75	5678.285714
8322	1.5	5548
8955	2.35	3810.638298
11996	2.33	5148.497854
7216	3	2405.333333
3659	1.9	1925.789474
24855	5	4971
74940		

Final data

SALES	AREA	SALES PER HECTARE
19847.00	1.75	£11,341.14
12877.00	1.50	£8,584.67
15813.00	2.35	£6,728.94
20819.00	2.33	£8,935.19
15016.00	3.00	£5,005.33
40655.00	5.00	£8,131.00
125027.00		

Formulae

SALES	AREA	SALES PER HECTARE
=SUM(B3:E3)	1.75	=F3/G3
=SUM(B4:E4)	1.5	=F4/G4
=SUM(B5:E5)	2.35	=F5/G5
=SUM(B6:E6)	2.33	=F6/G6
=SUM(B7:E7)	3	=F7/G7
=SUM(B8:E8)	5	=F8/G8
=SUM(F3:F8)		

Overall Totals

Databases

This unit introduces databases and shows how Access works. It includes adding, amending and deleting entries. It covers how to sort the database, create a search, save and print. It also covers database table creation.

Covers

Unit Five

The database

A database is simply a list of information. It should be organised in a logical way so that you can access the information easily and have a means for updating. An address book or the telephone directory is an example of a database that you use every day. The telephone directory is organised alphabetically and is updated annually.

A computerised database offers great flexibility. It allows you to add data, to edit or make changes to individual items promptly and to delete redundant data. It means you can manipulate the information, sort and find specific information quickly and easily.

Microsoft Excel

You could use a spreadsheet, such as Excel, to manage the database. It has many of the required functions. You can sort data easily,

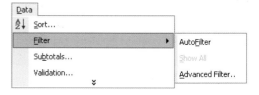

and search for specific data using the Filter function – indeed for a small database it may be the best choice, but it does have drawbacks. The spreadsheet is loaded into memory and works in memory. This may cause problems with large amounts of data. The spreadsheet format is not ideally suited to managing search or query results, especially when you have multiple queries. You are also susceptible to potential loss or corruption of data.

Microsoft Access

Access is a database program that is designed to work with large volumes of data. It writes the data to disk automatically as you work, so it is less likely to lose data. It allows you to perform all standard database activities in a controlled manner. It has tools and functions to manage input, editing, sorting and reports on the data. All these actions are carried out within the database file.

It allows you to input information into separate tables in the same database and link the tables. For example, in an employment database you could have three tables. One may contain personal information, such as address, marital status etc; one may have employment data such as payroll number, date started, NI number; and the third, assigned company car details. When you need information about an individual employee, you can link the tables.

This method of storing data along with the links between data elements is known as relational database, and the type of software that supports it is known as a relational database management system (RDBMS).

Start Access

 To start Access, select Start, All Programs, Microsoft Access.

 Until you create or open a database, only the New, Open and Search buttons are available. The remainder are inactive.

 Access uses the file extension .mdb.

 See page 120 if you wish to create your own database table.

 You can use File, Open, if the Task Pane is not available.

When you open Access, you are presented with a blank Database window and the Task Pane.

Title bar

Menu bar

Toolbar

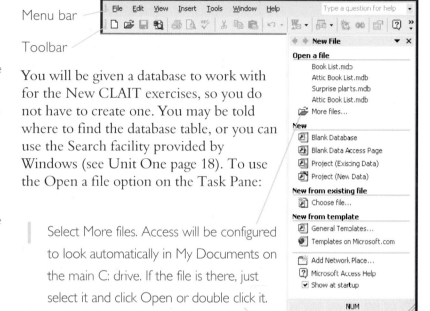

You will be given a database to work with for the New CLAIT exercises, so you do not have to create one. You may be told where to find the database table, or you can use the Search facility provided by Windows (see Unit One page 18). To use the Open a file option on the Task Pane:

1   Select More files. Access will be configured to look automatically in My Documents on the main C: drive. If the file is there, just select it and click Open or double click it.

2   If the file is in a different location, click the down arrow next to My Documents in the Look in bar, and navigate the drives and folders.

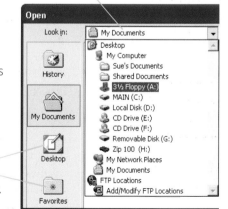

3   These icons present shortcuts to various locations on the computer.

4   When you open the file, it displays the main Database window.

The main database window

The main database window presents a series of objects or functions for you to use.

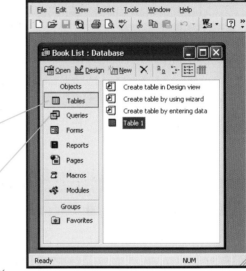

1 Tables. These contain the basic data of the database. In this database there is only one table and it is currently selected.

2 Queries. These are saved searches. You can look for specific information in the database, use complex criteria and save it for later re-use.

3 Forms. You can create custom forms for data input. Using forms can speed up data entry by filling in standard fields, such as today's date, department, etc., or by limiting the input to just some of the fields in the data table.

4 Reports. You can print data tables or queries in table format. Reports allow you to present the data in more readable or attractive way. You can use reports to create summary documents.

5 Pages are a means of sharing Access data across a network. Macros and Modules are complex features used by database programmers to create and run programs to perform a series of repetitive tasks. They use Visual Basic programming language.

Tables

The database table has a defined structure. Information is divided firstly into records. A record is all the information about an individual entry in the list, so for example in the telephone directory a record is name, initials, address, town and phone number for one person.

Within each record, the data is divided into fields.

FIELD 1 Surname	FIELD 2 Initials	FIELD 3 Address	FIELD 4 Town	FIELD 5 Phone No
Smith	J	1 The Highway	Anytown	01234-456789
Williams	J	2 London Road	Newtown	01222-333333

The type of information contained within each field is categorised. There are ten data types:

The data tables that you will use should only contain text, number, currency and date fields.

Text	text or combination of text and numbers
Memo	longer text entries
Number	numbers only, with or without decimals
Date/Time	date format 25/06/02 or 25-Jun-02
Currency	with £ or Euro
Autonumber	system generated to identify each record
Yes/No	logical, true/false, on/off
OLE Object	linked to an object elsewhere on PC
Hyperlink	linked to an object on a network
Lookup Wizard	create a link to another table

When the database table is created, the content of each field is assessed to determine the data type. By assigning each field a data type, a certain level of validation is achieved, for example, you cannot type text into a number field. When you use the tables created for you in the CLAIT exercises the data type is already set.

To open the table:

You must have the Tables tab selected to see the list of tables.

Select the table and double click the icon next to the table name (or press the Open button).

The tables you are given for practice may not have the ID autonumber field.

It is recommended database practice to have one, but not essential. It will not affect any activities in the database at New CLAIT level.

The database table is presented in datasheet view, the layout is very similar to a spreadheet. Each row contains one record and each record is divided into fields. The column headings show the field names.

Design view button

Number of records in database

Current record

Autonumber Field   Date Field   Currency Field

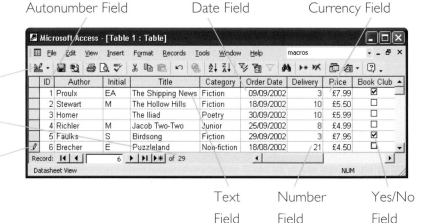

Text Field   Number Field   Yes/No Field

Access saves any data changes to disk automatically, without asking for confirmation.

Make sure that you do not change any data inadvertently.

2 You can move around the table using the scroll bars, the arrow keys or the Tab key.

3 Click in the Record indicator and type a number to go to that record. You can also select first, next in either direction or last.

Change column widths

You may also choose to narrow some columns, thus making more of the table visible at one time.

1 When you open the table, you may need to change some column widths to display all the data.

You must display all the data in a column. This is a New CLAIT course requirement.

2 Position the mouse on the divider between the column headings and drag to the desired width, or double click.

Editing the table

Add records

1. Click on the Add records button on the Toolbar.

   This positions the cursor at the end of the table. Just press Enter to skip the ID field, Access will enter that for you, and input the data.

2. As you enter the data, it is automatically written to disk. You do not have to save it.

Amend records

1. Just position the cursor on the data you wish to edit and retype.

2. The amendments are saved automatically.

Delete records

1. Select the record by clicking on the row heading.

	3	Homer		The Iliad
▶	4	Richler	M	Jacob Two-Tw
	5	Faulks	S	Birdsong

2. Click on the Delete record button on the Toolbar, or press the delete key. You will be warned that the deletion is permanent.

   Microsoft Access

   ⚠ You are about to delete 1 record(s).

   If you click Yes, you won't be able to undo this Delete operation. Are you sure you want to delete these records?

   [Yes]   [No]

3. You can delete a block of records.
   Select the first record, press and hold the Shift key, then click the last record of the block.

Find and replace

The Find and replace facility is used to update fields efficiently, especially when you need to replace the same data in many records.

The Find facility is just a subset of Find and Replace, and can be used in the same way.

1. Position your cursor in the column you are going to search. Select the Find button, or choose Edit, Replace from the menu.

2. Click the Replace tab to bring it to the front if necessary. Type in the data to Find, press tab and type in the Replace With data.

Match allows you to choose the whole field, or part of a field.

Leave Match Case unselected to look for all word forms, uppercase and lowercase.

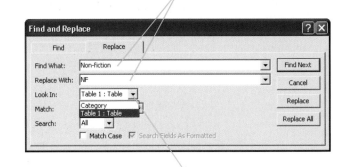

3. The Look In box allows you to limit the search to the current field, the quicker option, or to search the whole table. Search All means the whole column, rather than just from the cursor position.

It is better to restrict the Search to the one field, rather than search the whole table, so you don't get any unexpected results.

4. When you have chosen your options, select Find Next. The cursor moves to the next instance of the search item. To leave this instance, you can select Find Next again.

Replacing data cannot be Undone, since the changes are written to disk.

5. When you select Replace, the item is replaced and the cursor moves automatically to the next instance. Only select Replace All when you have replaced a few and are happy that the facility is working the way you expect.

Table tools

The Formatting toolbar is available but table presentation is not generally considered important. For presentation of data, you would use Forms and Reports.

The Access table has the Standard toolbar with some new buttons.

Sort Ascending/Descending

Filter by Selection/Form   Remove Filter

The sort facility works with numbers, dates, and logical fields as well as text. To sort the table:

You will always see a empty record at the bottom of the table. This record is not included when you sort or print.

1 Position the cursor anywhere in the column you wish to use as the primary sort key. Click on the A to Z to sort in ascending order. The Z to A is reverse sort order, which can be useful with numbers, sorting largest to smallest.

2 When you close the table, you will be asked if you wish to change the design. This relates simply to the re-sorted order of the table.

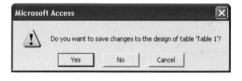

3 Click Yes if you wish to retain the order. However, there is very little advantage in saving the new order, as each time you use the table, you are likely to need to sort it again, either to incorporate new records or to use a different sorting field.

Two or more tables containing the same information may cause problems in managing the database, so Access does not allow it.

4 You cannot save the table under another name, though you can do so with other database objects.

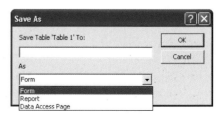

Criteria are used to identify which particular records you want to choose.

Filters on the database table allow you to select and search for data dynamically. The filter hides data that does not match your selected criteria. The toolbar provides two filters, Filter by Selection and Filter by Form.

To Filter by Selection:

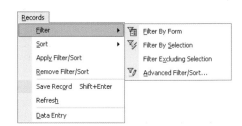

I Position your cursor in the field which contains your criteria.

2 Select Records, Filter, and Filter by Selection, or you can use the button on the toolbar.

You can print the selected records. Just click on the Print button.

3 The effect is to remove from view all records that do not match the data in the selected field.

Title	Category	Order Date
Cyclopaedia	NF	23/09/2002
Contract Bridge	NF	22/08/2002
Japan before Perry	NF	03/08/2002
Japanese Simplified	NF	03/08/2002
The Year I was Born	NF	24/07/2002
Marco Polo	NF	17/09/2002

When you apply a filter, you can still see all the information on each record. To see just certain fields in the result, you must use a Query.

4 To remove the filter, and see the complete datasheet once again, click the Remove Filter button, or select Records, Remove Filter/Sort.

The Filter by Form facility allows you to select on more than one criteria. It provides a structured form with drop-down lists for you to select fields and data values to define your criteria. To activate criterion, click on Apply filter. Click Close to return to the table.

Using Filter by Form is not recommended in the New CLAIT course.

Although Filter by Form remembers the filter criteria, you cannot save the search or results, or set any parameters on the search. For all of these activities you have to use an Access query.

Title	Category	Order Date	Delivery
	"NF"		
		24/07/2002	
		03/08/2002	
		14/08/2002	
		15/08/2002	
		16/08/2002	
		17/08/2002	
		18/08/2002	
		21/08/2002	

Queries

The Queries facility allows you to:

*   Search for records that match one or more criteria

*   View selected fields in the result

*   Save the query for re-use

Criteria can use complex relationships between fields in a record but for New CLAIT we only need the following types of criteria:

*   Matching text values in a field

*   Comparing number or date values

To compare use the following notation:

<table>
<tr><td><</td><td>Less than</td></tr>
<tr><td>></td><td>Greater than</td></tr>
<tr><td><=</td><td>Less than or equal to</td></tr>
<tr><td>>=</td><td>Greater than or equal to</td></tr>
</table>

To start a query and select the table:

It's a good idea to start off using the Design View method. You could use the Wizard to create the query, but it only helps you to select the fields, any more complex design features you must create yourself.

1 Select the Queries tab from the main database window.

2 Select Create query in Design view, and click on the Open button.

If we had several related tables in the database file, we could select more than one table at this point. We could create a query that requested information from several tables and brought the information together in one view. This is using Access as a relational database.

3 This displays the Show Table window. This window allows you to choose which table to use in the query. There is only one, already hightlighted, so just click Add and then Close.

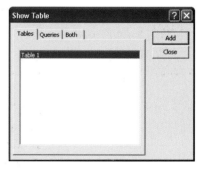

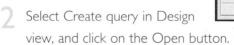

Create a query

1 When you select Add (see page 115) you will find the table appears in the top panel of the Query 1 window. It is provided to enable you to select the fields you want in your query.

2 To select the fields, you can double click the required field in the Table window, one at a time. This puts the field into the first and next empty column.

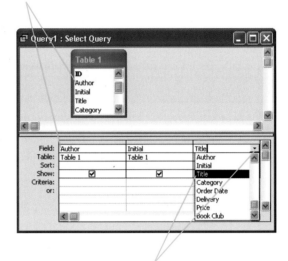

Avoid double clicking to insert a field into a column that is not visible, it looks like nothing has happened and you may end up with the same field selected twice.

3 Alternatively, click in the Field row, and select from the drop-down list. This is the easiest way to select fields if you need more than can be displayed at one time.

Build your query one step at a time. Select your fields, then run the query (see page 117). Return to the design and add one criterion, and run the query again. Return to the design and add another criterion if required, and so on. If at some point your query fails, then you know which step caused the problem.

4 Enter your criteria into the appropriate columns. The criteria illustrated

Field:	Title	Category	Price
Table:	Table 1	Table 1	Table 1
Sort:			
Show:	☑	☑	☑
Criteria:		"NF"	<=5
or:			

are NF for Category and less than or equal to £5.00 for price. Note that Access inserts the "" around NF to indicate a text entry, and that although Price is a currency field, you must not type the £ sign, or the query will not work correctly.

The CLAIT exercise will require you to use a criterion to select records, but not display that field when you run the query. For example, it may ask you to select non-fiction books, but not require you to include book category in the resulting table.

5 Run the query with the field included to check that the criteria has worked as expected, then return to the design view and de-select the Show box. It will not now display in the result.

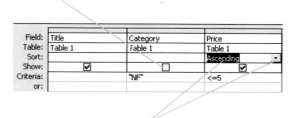

Field:	Title	Category	Price
Table:	Table 1	Table 1	Table 1
Sort:			Ascending
Show:	☑	☐	☑
Criteria:		"NF"	<=5
or:			

6 You may be required to present the results in a particular order. Select from the drop-down list in the appropriate column.

If you add more data to the original table, the next time you run the query new matching data will be added to the result.

When you have built the query as required, you can select either:

Run the Query   View Datasheet

To return to the Design view select:

To save the query:

You can open or save the query in datasheet view or design view.

Add your initials to the query name to identify it as yours if you have to share a printer.

7 Select File, Save. Supply a name that is relevant, and click on OK. The query is treated as an internal file in the database file.

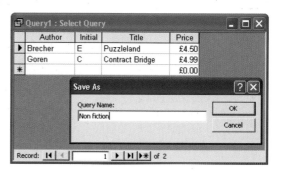

Printing tables and queries

New CLAIT only requires you to print the tables and queries in a table format. You do not have to use the Reports facility.

Printing in Access is less user-friendly than other Office programs. Each time you print you must check the setup because Access doesn't remember any previous requirements or changes to the default. To print a table or query:

1   Select your table or query and open it in the datasheet view. Click on Print Preview. The Status bar informs you if the print will take more than one page.

Page: |◄| ◄ | 1 | ► | ►|

2   If you need to change the paper orientation to landscape, select Setup. Click the Page tab to bring it to the fore and select the orientation you require.

You can print tables or queries without opening them, if you don't need to change anything. However, you can only access the Setup options through Print Preview, or if the table or query is open.

3   When you click OK you will return to the Preview window. Click on the Printer button and the document will be printed without need for further intervention.

Fit ▼ Close Setup

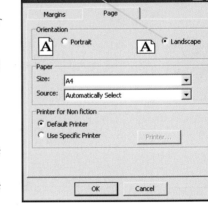

Always check the column widths on your printout to make sure that all the data is displayed.

Printing tables and queries in the datasheet view satisfies the New CLAIT course requirements. However, there is no header/footer option, or easy method for adding an identifying name. The columns of data often appear too close together and there are no alignment options. Where presentation is important, using the Report facility is recommended.

Try the Report wizard with a query that has only four or five columns to see how it works.

4   Select the Reports tab in the main database window. Choose Create report by using wizard. Follow the on-screen instructions a step at a time, and the report will be created and saved for you.

Close the database

When you start the next exercise, you must start a completely new database. Do not create another table within the same one.

By the time you have worked through a complete CLAIT exercise, you will have used a table and created several queries. You will have seen how an Access database contains all these objects, tables, queries, reports etc. within one database file. In Explorer only the .mdb file is visible. You cannot see the tables or queries that have been created and saved within it.

As explained earlier in the unit, you can have more than one table within the database file. However, when you start the next exercise you must start a completely new database. This is because these are separate exercises – you do not wish to create related tables.

Access is designed to prevent confusing tables within a database. When you open a new or second database, it automatically closes the first one.

When you close the database:

1 Close any open tables. Remember, any new or amended data will be saved automatically.

2 Save and close any open queries, if not previously saved. You are saving the design of the query, not the data. If you add more records to your table, the next time you run your query, the results may be different.

3 Close the database file. You will not be prompted to save it, or need to save it.

If you use Excel to create your database, you will need to save the file. Any new or amended data must be saved. In Excel, when you create and run a query, the resulting report is written within the spreadsheet. This will be saved with the spreadsheet, and must be erased before the query can be run again. If you create several queries, managing the resulting reports can be quite difficult.

Create your own table

Knowing how to build a database table will be useful, especially if you decide to take a further course. It is quite a simple process, and provides further information on how the database works.

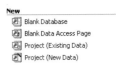

1 Open Access. From the Task Pane select New, Blank database.

2 You now are requested to name the file and save it. Access saves the file first so that it can write data to disk as you type it in. When you have selected the destination folder and supplied the name, click Create.

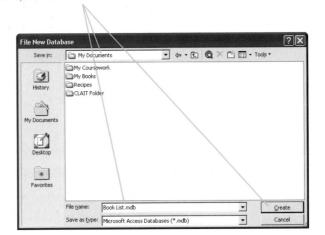

3 The main database window will be displayed with the Tables tab selected.

4 You could use Create table by using wizard. This takes you a step at a time through creating a table using pre-defined templates.

5 However, to maintain complete control over the design process, select Create table in Design view.

6 The Table Design view window presents three columns. In the Field Name column type the text that will become the column heading. Press Enter or tab and move to the Data Type cell.

See page 109 for more detail on data types.

7 In the Data Type cell click the drop-down list and select from the available data types.

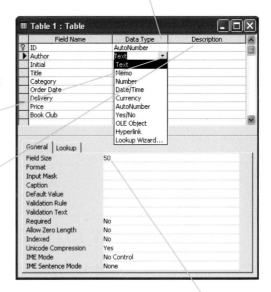

8 The Description area allows for design comments. It does not need to be completed.

Long integer means whole numbers. You must select single or double to use decimal values.

9 The Field Properties area allows you to select the finer details of how the data can be controlled. For example in a text field, the default field size is 50 characters. In a numeric field you can control the field size, format and decimal places.

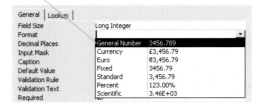

Creating a primary key adds an ID field to the database table and allows you to create a relationship between tables in the database.

10 When you have completed the design, select File, Save and save the table. You will be prompted to provide a primary key. Click Yes to create the ID field. Close the design view and open in datasheet view to input data. When you open the table you will see the field headings at the top of the table.

Exercise

You are allowed two hours to complete this assignment.

Scenario

Your Supervisor has asked you to maintain a database of plants and provide reports when required. If you are using this book for self study, and have downloaded the data files, you'll find the Access file for the Surprise Plants database in the Unit 5 DB folder.

The New CLAIT in easy steps data files may be downloaded from the In Easy Steps Web site (see page 233). Use the .mdb file for Access 2002 or Access 2000. If you have an older version of Access you can create a new database table following the steps in the file Create_Database.txt.

1. Open the Surprise Plants Database.
    The Plant section manager has decided to add four new plants to the list, and remove from sale one plant that does not grow well in this area.

2. Create records for the new plants as follows:

    The PYRACANTHA is a SHRUB, colour WHITE. It flowers in SPRING at a height of 350 cms. It will be available from 01/02/02, price £7.50.

    The VERBASCUM is a PERENNIAL, colour YELLOW. It flowers in SUMMER, grows to 125 cms. It will be available from 25/04/02, price £3.75.

    The ASTER is a PERENNIAL, colour BLUE. It flowers in SUMMER, grows to 40 cms. It will be available from 18/04/02, price £2.75.

    The GEUM is a PERENNIAL, colour ORANGE. It flowers in AUTUMN, grows to 45 cms. It will be available from 01/06/02, price £3.50.

It has been decided not to sell the CANNA. Delete the record for CANNA.

3. Using codes for TYPE would be more efficient. Replace the existing data as follows:
    Replace PERENNIAL with PE
    Replace SHRUB with SH
    Replace BULB with BU

4. Print all of the data in table format.

5. Some of the data needs to be amended.
    The SEDUM is BRONZE
    The PRIMROSE is 10 cms high
    Make these changes and ensure the amended data is saved.

The Plant Sales Department would like to create a leaflet listing plants for a Spring Garden.

6. Set up the following database query:
    Select all plants that flower in the SPRING.
    Sort them into alphabetical order of NAME.
    Display only NAME, COLOUR and HEIGHT.
    Save the query and print it in table format.

The Landscape Department wants a list of winter flowering plants.

7. Set up the following database query:
    Select all plants that bloom in WINTER, with a height of 50cms or more.
    Sort the list in ascending order of HEIGHT.
    Display only NAME, HEIGHT and PRICE.
    Save the query and print it in table format.

The Surprise Gardening Club would like to plan a budget garden.

8. Set up the following database query:
    Select all plants that cost less than £4.00
    Sort into order of AVAILABLE
    Print NAME, COLOUR , SEASON and HEIGHT.
    Save the query and print in table format.

9. Close the file and exit the database with all the data saved.

Checklist

When you have finished the exercise, use the following checklist. Have you:

- Added the new records, made the amendments and deleted records correctly
- Created queries and checked the results
- Saved the queries
- Printed the table and queries and ensured that the data printed correctly without losing any data

Answers

NAME	TYPE	COLOUR	SEASON	HEIGHT	AVAILABLE	PRICE
CAMPANULA	PE	WHITE	SPRING	35	01/03/2002	£1.50
HOSTA	PE	GREY	SUMMER	15	20/03/2002	£3.65
LAVATERA	SH	PINK	SUMMER	150	25/04/2002	£5.99
OXALIS	PE	PINK	WINTER	15	01/10/2002	£2.50
SEDUM	PE	RED	AUTUMN	40	02/04/2002	£1.75
LILIUM	BU	CREAM	SUMMER	100	20/03/2002	£2.75
HYDRANGEA	SH	BLUE	SUMMER	150	25/04/2002	£4.95
IRIS	BU	BLUE	SPRING	25	01/03/2002	£0.95
HELLEBORUS	PE	GREEN	WINTER	50	01/10/2002	£2.80
PRIMROSE	PE	YELLOW	SPRING	20	10/10/2002	£0.65
DAFFODIL	BU	YELLOW	SPRING	40	01/09/2002	£0.10
AZALEA	SH	BLUE	SPRING	50	01/02/2002	£3.95
BEGONIA	BU	YELLOW	SUMMER	35	01/03/2002	£0.75
VIBURNUM	SH	PINK	WINTER	200	01/09/2002	£6.95
DAPHNE	SH	MAUVE	WINTER	100	10/10/2002	£4.95
PYRACANTHA	SH	WHITE	SPRING	350	01/02/2002	£7.50
VERBASCUM	PE	YELLOW	SUMMER	125	25/04/2002	£3.75
ASTER	PE	BLUE	SUMMER	40	18/04/2002	£2.75
GEUM	PE	ORANGE	AUTUMN	45	01/06/2002	£3.50

Print 1

NAME	COLOUR	HEIGHT
AZALEA	BLUE	50
CAMPANULA	WHITE	35
DAFFODIL	YELLOW	40
IRIS	BLUE	25
PRIMROSE	YELLOW	10
PYRACANTHA	WHITE	350

Print 2

NAME	HEIGHT	PRICE
HELLEBORUS	50	£2.80
DAPHNE	100	£4.95
VIBURNUM	200	£6.95

Print 3

NAME	COLOUR	SEASON	HEIGHT
AZALEA	BLUE	SPRING	50
BEGONIA	YELLOW	SUMMER	35
IRIS	BLUE	SPRING	25
CAMPANULA	WHITE	SPRING	35
LILIUM	CREAM	SUMMER	100
HOSTA	GREY	SUMMER	15
SEDUM	BRONZE	AUTUMN	40
ASTER	BLUE	SUMMER	40
VERBASCUM	YELLOW	SUMMER	125
GEUM	ORANGE	AUTUMN	45
DAFFODIL	YELLOW	SPRING	40
HELLEBORUS	GREEN	WINTER	50
OXALIS	PINK	WINTER	15
PRIMROSE	YELLOW	SPRING	10

Print 4

Desktop publishing

In this unit you will learn how to produce simple publications using imported text and image files. It includes managing page layout, moving and resizing text and images, saving and printing.

Covers

Unit Six

Desktop publishing

Creating a document for publication used to be restricted to the complex skills of the trained typesetter. The mixing of text and pictures of varying styles and sizes into an attractive and acceptable format took time and expertise.

With the advent of the latest computers, and their powerful hardware and sophisticated software, desktop publishing has become available to most computer users. We are able to move and resize objects with just the press of a mouse button and we can view the work in progress and make amendments very easily.

Most of the text editing skills that you learnt in Word can be used in Publisher.

Word vs Publisher

To create a publication, we could use either a word processor, or a desktop publishing program. Word processors today have great functionality. Word, in particular, allows us to work with text and images together on the same page. We can resize and move both text and images. We can draw lines, boxes and other shapes, and we can layer and group objects. In fact, at the beginner level, as required in the New CLAIT course, we could use Word as our desktop publishing program. However, many of these are secondary functions, harder to access and not so easy to use. The layout and placement of text on the page is controlled by margins, tabs and breaks and has little flexibility.

A full DTP program, however, provides all this function and more but with greater ease of use. The Publisher desktop, for example, is larger than a standard sheet of A4 paper, and can be used as a holding area for text and pictures, much as you would use a real desk top. In a desktop publishing package, the text is restricted to the text box, whatever its size, and the text box is treated as an object that can be placed anywhere on the page, moved or resized. Many of Publisher's facilities reflect the finer details of publishing, such as layout guides and aligning to a grid. There are commercial printing tools, and the facility to create special printouts with colour requisites.

It is often better to create paragraphs of text in Word, where you can make editing changes easily. Then copy and paste them into text boxes in Publisher to place them on the page.

Publisher has a design wizard to help you through the steps involved in creating quite complex publications. It provides templates for you to select from, if you need suggestions or help with designs and layouts, and it can work with varying paper sizes and orientation.

Start Publisher

If you are using Windows XP, after you have opened Publisher a few times, it will appear on the first level of the Start menu.

To open Microsoft Publisher:

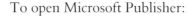

1   Select Start, All programs, Microsoft Publisher. This will open the Publisher window with the New Publisher task pane. If the task pane doesn't appear automatically, select File, New. The task pane displays the publication Wizard design categories..

It can be useful before you start the CLAIT exercise to use the wizard to create a publication just to see how Publisher works.

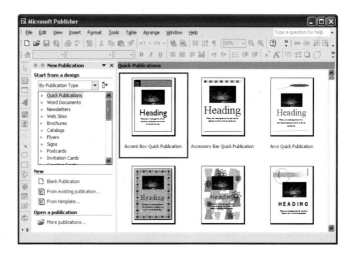

2   Click the button to display the Publication Gallery, if it's not already visible. This illustrates the publications in the selected category, in this case Quick Publications. Scroll the Preview pane to see the other designs in the category, or click on a different category to view those types of publication.

The Open a Publication section takes you to the Open file window to access files already created. It will also list recently created publications.

3   You'd click the down arrow and choose Publications by Design, to select a layout for a fax cover, label, calendar etc. based on a colour and logo concept, providing a consistent house style for your publications.

4   Select the Blank Publications tab to start with a fresh sheet.

The Publisher window

1 The Blank Publications gallery shows a variety of paper formats and dimensions. Click a page type to start a publication.

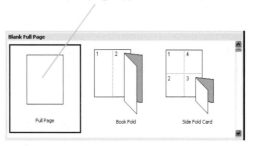

If the task pane does not show when you open Publisher, you will start at this point.

2 This closes the Gallery and reveals a standard sheet of A4 paper, your blank working page. The blue and pink lines are non-printing lines, referred to as layout guides, that indicate the default margins.

To show Tool tips, the purpose of each tool, select View, Toolbars, Options, and tick Show ScreenTips on toolbars.

The Publisher Objects toolbar is usually displayed vertically. However, it can be moved to a different location, like the other toolbars.

Menu bar
Standard toolbar
Objects toolbar
Select Objects
Text Box
Insert Table
Insert Word Art
Picture Frame
Clip Art Frame

Drawing Tools
AutoShapes
Web Page Tools

Design Gallery object
Vertical Ruler

Object Size
Object Position
Page Navigation

Create a page layout

The standard page size for all documents in the UK is A4, paper orientation is normally Portrait, i.e. upright. To change the page orientation in Publisher:

1 Select File, Page Setup, and choose landscape.

2 The paper dimensions are shown, with a preview pane and layout notes.

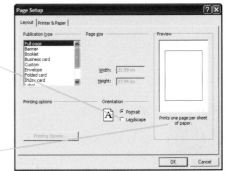

Layout guides, the blue and pink lines, are set initially to define the working area and the page margins. The CLAIT exercise requires specific margin sizes, which may be different from the default.

To view the current settings and if necessary set new layout guides:

1 Select from the menu bar, Arrange, Layout Guides.

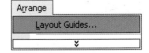

2 Use the arrows or type in the boxes to adjust the positions of the Margin guides as required.

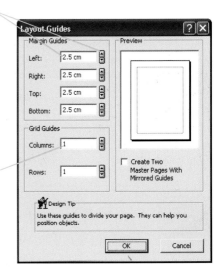

3 Specifying the number of columns in the Margin guides may be helpful, especially if you use Connected Text Boxes for multicolumn text (see page 133).

Templates

In this initial template only the margin guides have been set. You can create templates that have complex layouts with gridlines, logos and other items included.

Having created the required page layout, with margin guides, you can save it as a Template. Creating a template means that this layout can be used repeatedly, you just need to select which template to use when you start. To save as a Template:

If you continue to work when you have saved your template, you must use Save As to rename the exercise and save it as a regular Publisher file or it will overwrite your template.

1   Select File, Save As. Click on the down arrow on the Save as type box and change the file type to a Publisher Template.

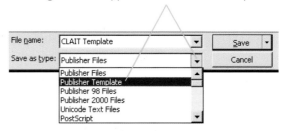

Note, it's easiest to use the Task Pane to access the Templates. They are saved into a subfolder deep in the folder system, and are not easily found.

2   The Save in folder changes automatically to the Templates folder. You may see other Templates listed. Type in the file name and click on Save. Note that the template keeps the .pub file extension, the same as the normal file extension for Publisher documents.

To use a saved or existing Template:

To access Templates in previous versions of Publisher, click the Templates button at the bottom of the Wizard panel.

3   Select File, New. This opens the Publisher Task Pane and Publication Gallery (see page 127). At the foot of the task pane, select New, From Template.

Create New creates a new document, not another template.

4   This opens the Templates folder, and displays the available templates. Select the template name and click Create New.

Frames and boxes

Many of the Publisher tools deal with Frames which are containers for images, clip art and tables. Text is created or imported into a Text Box, also known as a Text Frame (the term used in previous versions of Publisher). DTP is in essence the management and manipulation of these frames and boxes.

To create a Text Box:

1 Select the Text Box tool, by clicking on it and letting go. Move the mouse to the page area and the arrow becomes a large **+ (plus)**, also known as Cross-hairs.

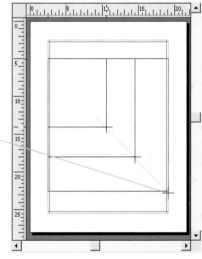

2 Position the centre of the cross-hairs on the outer margin guide. Hold down the left mouse button, and drag down and across diagonally.

3 Release the mouse button, and Selection Handles appear at the corners and on the sides of the box. There are similar Selection Handles for an active picture frame.

4 To resize, position the mouse over a selection handle and you will get an arrow indicating the direction in which you will resize:

Horizontally Vertically Diagonally

5 To move a frame, position the mouse pointer on the edge of the frame. It will change to the four-headed cross symbol, with a moving van. Just press the left mouse button and drag to the required location.

6 To delete a text box, press Shift+Delete. Pressing just Delete will delete the selected text within the box. To delete a picture frame, select the frame and press the Delete key.

Text box layout

For the heading text box you will need to create a separate frame, which will be the full page width, and its depth will be dependant on the size of font you choose.

The body text, which is the imported text file, will occupy much of the page and must be laid out in two or more columns as in a newletter. To create a column layout in one text box:

1 Click in the main or body text box. Select Format Text Box from the menu, click the Text Box tab, and press the Columns button.

2 Choose the number of columns. The Preview panel shows you the results of your choice. Columns created this way are sure to be equal in width.

3 The Spacing box allows you to specify the column gutter or space between the text in adjacent columns. The amount selected is shared between the columns.

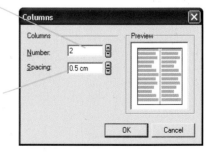

Connected frames

An alternative to creating one text box with two or more columns is to create a number of text boxes the same size and connect them.

If you don't see the Connect Frames toolbar, select Views, Toolbars and click Connect Frames.

1 Create a series of text boxes on the page. For New CLAIT they must be the same width so you can use the column guide to help, or you can copy and paste the first frame, which is much easier.

You must keep your column widths equal. If you need to resize one frame to accommodate text, you must resize the others.

2 Select the first frame, so the selection handles appear. Click on the Create Text Box Link button on the Connect Frames toolbar.

3 The mouse pointer becomes a pitcher or jug, and will tip when you move it into the second text box. Click to complete the connection. The frames are now linked, and when you import text it will flow from one frame to the next.

If you forget to connect the frames together before you import the text file, and the text will overflow, Publisher will offer to connect the frames for you. See page 135 for Text in overflow.

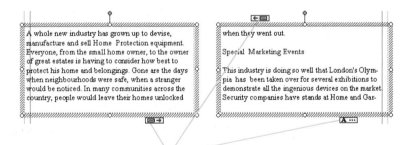

4 You'll see a link indicator at the bottom of the first text box. Click on the link to move to the next text box. The last text box has a link indicator at the top, connecting back to the previous box. If the text overflows the combined boxes, there's an indicator at the bottom.

You must also ensure that the column gutter is correct, as no tolerance is allowed. Remember that Publisher allows 1 mm between the text and each frame so include this in your calculations.

5.500, 8.500 cm.   4.000 x 4.500 cm.

5 To set the size and spacing of frames you will need to use the Object Position and Object Size indicators on the Status bar.

Import text

You can type text into a text box, or you can use text created in another application and import it. In the CLAIT exercise you will type the heading into the heading frame, but import the text into the main text box. This is because the emphasis is on the placement and management of the text.

To import the text:

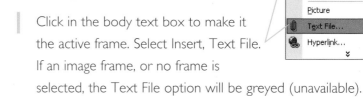

1 Click in the body text box to make it the active frame. Select Insert, Text File. If an image frame, or no frame is selected, the Text File option will be greyed (unavailable).

2 The Insert Text dialog box opens the My Documents folder. Navigate the folders if necessary to find the text file. It shows files of all text

formats, including Publisher and Word, so you could change File Type to Plain text to make your file easier to locate.

3 When you have found the file, click OK.

4 The text will be inserted into the frame, and will flow into both columns.

5 Note that if your text box is not large enough, you will get a warning message. See page 135.

Text in overflow

When you import text you may not be sure how big the text box needs to be. The amount of text and the font size are the critical factors.

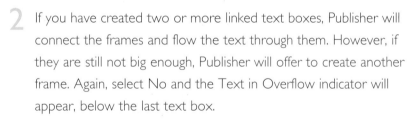

Frames and boxes in Publisher are easily resized, you don't need to get the size right the first time.

1 If the text box is too small, you will be warned that the inserted text doesn't fit the frame. If you have created one frame, click on No. The text will be placed into the box, flow through the columns if specified, and the Text in Overflow indicator will appear at the bottom.

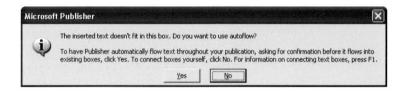

2 If you have created two or more linked text boxes, Publisher will connect the frames and flow the text through them. However, if they are still not big enough, Publisher will offer to create another frame. Again, select No and the Text in Overflow indicator will appear, below the last text box.

Once you have all the text showing, it's a good idea to make a note of the last few words of the text, just to make sure that they are showing when you print.

3 All you have to do is keep stretching the text box or frames, resizing until the frame is big enough and the symbol disappears.

To keep the text box the same size, click in the box, select Format Text Box, Text Box and choose Best Fit. The font size will be adjusted so that the text just fits.

4 The Text in Overflow symbol may appear when you resize the body text font, or when you move and resize images.

5 It also may appear when you enter text in a very large font size into the heading frame. Again, just stretch the frame, or shrink the text.

Fonts

Font styles

For the New CLAIT course, you are required to use two different font styles, serif and sans serif fonts.

1. Serif fonts are those fonts where the letters have a stroke across the bottom of the letter. The standard serif font is Times New Roman.

Times New Roman Serif Font

2. Sans serif fonts are those where there is no line at the base. The standard suggested font is Arial.

Arial Sans Serif Font

3. To use a particular font, create the text box and select the style before you type. Alternatively, type the text in the default font, select the text and then apply the required font style.

4. Publisher will list the styles in the Font Schemes task pane. The fonts are named using their own type faces and they are displayed in groups that look good together.

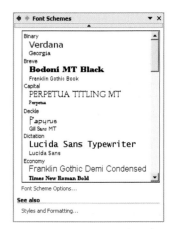

Font Sizes

You will be required to display three differing sizes of text, a main heading size, a subheading size and a body text size. If the exact font size is not given, choose from these ranges:

Body text	–	10 to 14 point
Subheading	–	16 to 18 point
Main heading	–	24 to 28 point

Text alignment

The required text alignment will vary from frame to frame. The heading text, which you type in, will need to be centred across both columns and reach from margin to margin. The body text alignment will be changed during the exercise to demonstrate control. The alignment buttons are the same as used in Word. See page 45 for more details. To apply the alignment:

1 Click in each paragraph and select the required alignment. It will be applied to the whole paragraph.

2 Press Ctrl+A to select everything within the text box, and then select the alignment. Be careful if the alignment for the subheadings should be different.

You will be required to indent part of the text. This means moving the first line or a whole paragraph, whichever is specified, to the right. To indent text:

3 Position the cursor in the paragraph that you need to indent. Select Format, Indents and Lists.

4 For a first line indent click on the up arrow to the required amount, or type the value into the box. You will see a preview in the Sample pane. You can also use this dialog box to set paragraph alignment and line spacing.

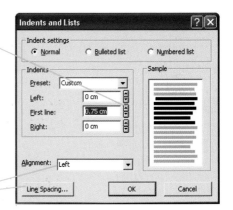

Import an image file

Use Publisher's Help facility to see all the picture file formats you can import into Publisher. Search for "graphics file formats and filters".

Publisher allows you to insert both Clip Art images and images from other sources into your publication. It provides two separate buttons and menu entries, the Clip Art option opens the Clip Organizer, and the Picture from File opens the My Pictures folder. To import a picture file:

Picture frame

Clip Organizer

Frame

1 Select the Picture Frame button. Move the mouse pointer to the page area where it becomes crosshairs. Position the mouse where you want the image, hold down the left mouse button and draw a box frame (initially square).

To insert a Clip Art image, select the Clip Organizer Frame button to display the Insert Clip Art task pane, and search for an image. When you Insert the image, a clip art frame is created automatically.

2 Choose Insert, Picture, From File. My Pictures folder will open. You may need to browse the folders to find the image file.

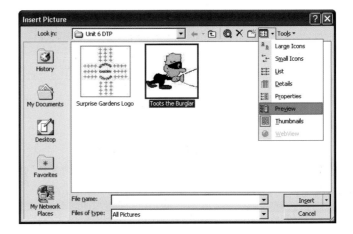

To help in selecting the correct image, use the Preview facility.

The image can be adjusted if it is the wrong size or in the wrong location. See page 139.

3 Click on Insert and the image will be inserted into the frame. The image will be resized to fit the frame width. The frame height will be adjusted to keep the correct proportions. Note that if you had just clicked the page, instead of drawing a frame, the image will be inserted full size.

Image management

When you first start the CLAIT exercise, read it through and take particular notice of how you will need to change the image. If you are asked to make it bigger, start with a small image, and vice versa.

The frame automatically adjusts to the correct ratio when you insert the image the first time, whatever shape frame you created.

Select the wrapping style that meets the requirements of the exercise. Usually this will be Square, or Top and bottom:

When you have column text, make sure that the image is no more than the width of a column.

To resize an image:

1 Use the white selection handle on any corner, not on the sides. Dragging the corner handles maintains the proportions.

To move an image:

2 Position the mouse pointer on any edge, avoiding the selection handles. When it changes to the Moving van symbol, drag to the required position.

To rotate an image:

3 Hold the mouse over the green Rotation handle until it changes, then click and drag to the required angle. Press Shift to rotate 15 degrees at a time.

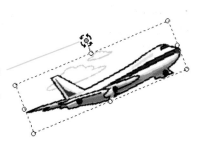

To fit an image to text:

4 When you place an image in a Text Box, tell Publisher how to arrange the text. Select Format Picture from the Picture toolbar, choose the Layout tab, and click the Wrapping Style you'd like to use. In this example, Top and bottom has been selected.

Security Devices

The result has been a boom in the sales of special locks and safes. There is also a growing

interest in electronic gadgetry designed to scare off burglars. Security alarms are very popular, and discourage the opportunist.

Drawing tools

You can use the Line Tool to draw a line under the heading, or between two columns of text. You can use the Rectangle Tool to draw a box around the heading or image. You can also use the Frame Border option, see page 141.

To use the drawing tools, select the tool and move to the page area. Position the crosshairs where you wish to begin, and just drag to draw the shape. Shapes can be resized and moved just like images and text boxes.

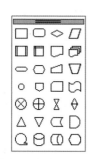

1 The Line Tool draws a line between any two points. To keep to a strict horizontal, vertical or 45 degree angle, hold down the Shift key as you drag.

2 The Arrow tool also draws a line, but adds an arrow head at one end or both ends.

3 The Oval Tool draws an oval, and makes it a true circle if you hold down the Shift key whilst dragging.

4 The Rectangle Tool draws a box, which will be an exact square if you hold down Shift as you drag.

The contents of the Formatting and Picture toolbars change, depending on which type of object has been selected.

5 Click on AutoShapes to draw stars, banners, U-turns and many other shapes, just like AutoShapes in Word (see page 178).

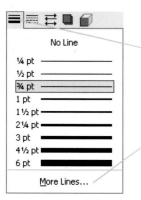

6 Click the shape and choose Line from the Picture toolbar, to pick thickness and line style.

7 Click on More Lines to see the complete range of options and select a dashed line style, or change the line colour. Click OK to apply the changes.

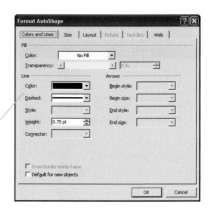

Borders

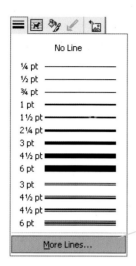

To put a border around a text or image frame:

1 Select the Line/Border Style button from the Picture toolbar, and pick a line style and width. Notice that the selection offered is greater than for AutoShapes (see page 140).

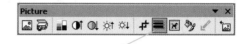

2 For more choice and greater control, select More Lines (or click Format Picture on the Picture toolbar).

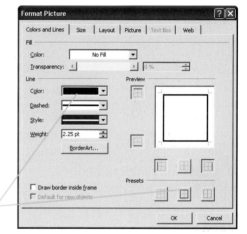

You will find more border styles in the Clip Art Organizer.

3 To put a border around the whole object select Box and then the colour and thickness. You will see the effect in the Preview panel.

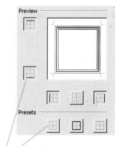

4 For a special effect, click the Border Art button, and select a picture that will be replicated as a border on all four sides of the selected object.

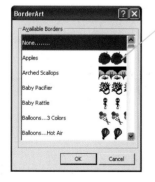

5 To put a border on just one edge, first select the None option. This will cancel any previous selection. Then select the edge you want and reselect colour and thickness. You can use this method to draw a line under the heading.

Final publication layout

The finished publication must always meet the requirements of the CLAIT exercise.

A degree of variation between presentations is expected as image sizes and choice of heading and subheading font sizes can affect the publication layout. The final step is to balance the columns so that each column finishes at about the same point on the page. Publisher has a Line Spacing facility that allows you to fine tune the spacing, making it easier to achieve a balanced page.

Three sizes of font, heading, subheading and body text, must be obviously discernable. Your choice of Serif and Sans Serif fonts must clearly display the difference in style.

1 Press Ctrl+A to select all the text, then click Format, Line Spacing.

Make sure that the text does not overflow the text box when you change the paragraph spacing.

2 You will need to experiment with the various spacings to achieve the balanced columns and full page layout requirement. A tolerance of two lines difference in column length is accepted.

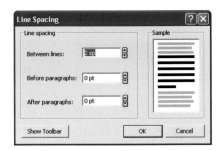

The Design Checker

Publisher provides the Design Checker to examine your finished document to help with some of these items.

The Design Checker does not check your margins for you.

1 Select Tools, Design Checker, and the options button. Tick the items to check.

You can work with the document to correct problems whilst this dialog box is still open.

2 When you run the Design Checker, it identifies problems and offers solutions and explanations.

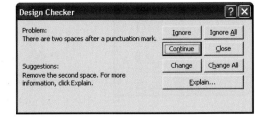

Printing publications

You are required for the New CLAIT course to print a composite publication. Put simply, it just means producing a print that shows all the elements of the finished item. Professional printing companies would require a composite and a series of colour separation prints. These show the breakdown of individual colours onto separate printing plates. Publisher has Commercial Printing Tools that allow you to print to commercial specifications.

1 Select Tools, Commercial Printing Tools, Colour Printing to see the options.

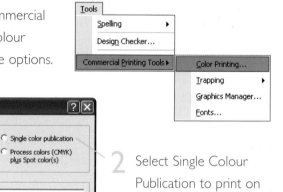

2 Select Single Colour Publication to print on a monochrome printer, and print in black and greyscales.

3 Using the normal File, Print, will produce the composite print, which is the format required for CLAIT exercises.

4 To print the text part of the publication for proofreading, select File, Print, and click the Advanced Print Settings button. Choose Do not print any graphics and it will put placeholders on the page.

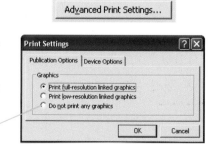

Exercise

You are allowed two hours to complete this exercise.

Scenario

You are working as an administrative assistant at Surprise Garden Centres headquarters. Your task it to create an advertisement for Surprise Garden Centres.

1. Create a new single-page publication.

2. Set up the master page or template for the page as follows:
    Page size   A4
    Page orientation   landscape
    Top/bottom margins   2 cms
    Left/right margins   2.5 cms

3. Save the master/template

4. Set up the page layout in a newsletter format, to include a page wide heading above three columns of text.
    Column widths   equal
    Space between columns   0.75 cm

5. Enter the heading SURPRISE GARDENS at the top of the page using a sans serif font.

6. Increase the size of the heading text so that is extends across the full width of all the columns of text.

Find the text file in the Unit 6 DTP folder, in the New CLAIT in easy steps data files downloaded from the In Easy Steps Web site (see page 233).

7. Import the text file Surprise Garden Centres so that it begins at the top of the left hand column, below the heading.

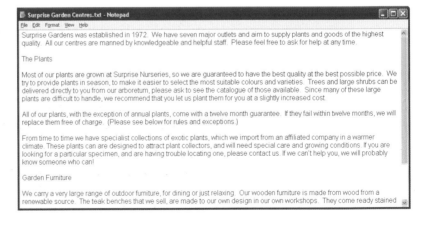

You'll also find the image file in the Unit 6 DTP folder, in the New CLAIT in easy steps data files.

8. Format the body text to be left-aligned, in a serif font.

9. Import the image Surprise Gardens Rose.tif, and place it at the bottom of the right-hand column, against the right margin line, making sure that it does not cover any text.

10. Print one composite proof copy of the publication for your manager. Make sure that the printed publication fits onto one page.

You have been asked to make the following amendments:

11. Draw a single border around the three columns of text and the graphic. Make sure that the border does not overlap any text. Your border may extend into the margin area.

12. Increase the size of the subheadings, The Plants, Garden Furniture and Summerhouses and Conservatories, so that they are larger than the body text, but smaller than the page heading.

13. Make the image smaller, and move it higher up the page, and across to the left hand column, just below the first paragraph. Arrange it so that the column text is above and below only. Make sure that the image does not extend into the margin.

14. Change the body text to be fully justified, in a serif font.

15. Format the body text so that the first line of each paragraph is indented. Make sure that the subheadings are not indented.

16. Increase the size of the body text so that the columns are balanced at the bottom of the page. Make sure that the headings, subheadings and body text are still different sizes.

17. Save and print a composite proof of the publication. Make sure that your printed publication fits on one page.

18. Close the publication and exit the software correctly.

Checklist

When you have finished the exercise, use the following checklist. Have you:

- Created a template using the publication
- Created text boxes at the required locations
- Inserted or typed text as specified
- Inserted the image in the proper position
- Printed the file and saved it
- Amended text format and alignment as requested
- Resized and repositioned the image
- Adjusted the text sizes to balance the columns
- Ensured that there is no text missing or covered
- Saved and printed the revised publication

Answers

Print 1

Print 2

Graphs and charts

This unit covers using Excel to create a series of graphs and charts. It includes creating pie, bar and line graphs, controlling presentation of the data and scale, managing and printing the graphs.

Covers

Unit Seven

Chart programs in Office

Charting data is a very good way to highlight particular trends or patterns. It makes comparison of data much simpler, and can make the data easier to explain and understand. Charts provide an important visual element to reports, helping to make them more interesting and professional.

Microsoft Excel

Excel is the natural choice for creating graphs and charts in the Microsoft Office suite. Excel offers the largest choice of chart styles and provides the greatest level of control over how the data is presented. It provides a wizard to take you step by step through a complex process and allows you a preview of the chart created at every step. Headings, labels and legends can be added as you proceed. Once the chart has been created, final amendments and modifications are simplified as each element of the chart can be accessed independently.

The Graph program

Microsoft Office provides a generic graph program which is used by several of the applications. You can create a table in Word, and invoke the Graph program to construct a quick and simple graph to illustrate your data. You can then delete the original table and just show the data in graphed format.

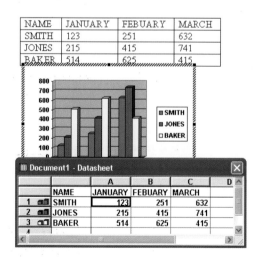

The same Graph program is used in Access to insert a chart into a report, and again in PowerPoint for a presentation.

Chart types

Each type of graph or chart has its own particular strengths for illustrating data.

Column chart – compares one or more types of data on a vertical axis, accepted by New CLAIT as a bar chart

Bar chart – compares one or more types of data on a horizontal axis

Line graph – shows up and down movement and trend over time

The exercise will tell you which chart to use, so you just need to follow instructions.

Pie chart – compares relative values of parts to a whole item or collection

XY Scatter graph – shows the relationship between two related data types

Area graph – illustrates the relative importance of values over time

These are most of the standard graphs offered in Excel. Others include Radar, Cylinder, Cone and Pyramid. There are also a multitude of Custom Types provided in the Chart Wizard.

Doughnut chart – like a pie chart, but may contain more than one series

Bubble graph – similar to a scatter graph, identifies clusters of values

Stock chart – with both line and column entries, this is designed especially to highlight stock market trends

Parts of a chart

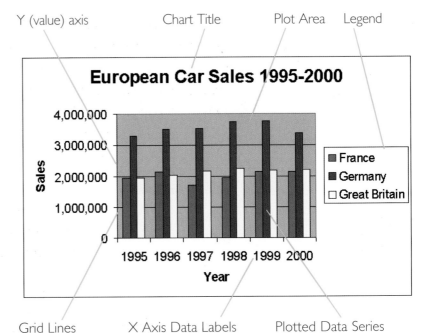

Y (value) axis   Chart Title   Plot Area   Legend

Grid Lines   X Axis Data Labels   Plotted Data Series

The plotted figures are the data series. Excel will use the row labels as the series names.

Chart title	–	will be keyed in as part of the exercise
Plot area	–	the background to the columns or lines
Legend	–	table identifying each column or data series
X axis	–	the identifying axis with data labels
Y axis	–	shows the value or quantity
Grid lines	–	indicate stages or values at regular intervals
Axis labels	–	will be keyed in as part of the exercise

The Chart data

You will be provided with a spreadsheet containing the necessary data. Creating graphs from a datasheet works best when there are no blank columns or rows in the data, so if there are any, it's a good idea to delete them before you start.

You can chart just a subset of the rows and columns of your data. For example, the chart above just uses three rows.

	A	B	C	D	E	F	G
1	European Car Sales 1995 - 2000 (units)						
2	Country	Year 1	Year 2	Year 3	Year 4	Year 5	Year 6
3	France	1,930,504	2,132,091	1,713,030	1,943,553	2,148,423	2,133,884
4	Germany	3,314,061	3,496,320	3,528,179	3,740,339	3,787,679	3,382,482
5	Great Britain	1,945,365	2,025,450	2,170,725	2,247,403	2,197,615	2,221,670
6	Italy	1,731,447	1,732,189	2,411,900	2,364,200	2,349,200	2,415,600
7	Netherlands	446,416	473,473	478,318	543,112	611,767	597,638

Create a pie chart

1 Select the data you wish to graph. You can include the title, and the row and column headings. Remember, cell A1 contains all the title text and is the first selected cell in the range, so remains white.

	A	B	C	D
1	European Car Sales	1995 - 2000 (u		
2	Country	Year 1	Year 2	Year 3
3	France	1,930,504	2,132,091	1,713,030
4	Germany	3,314,061	3,496,320	3,528,179
5	Great Britain	1,945,365	2,025,450	2,170,725
6	Italy	1,731,447	1,732,189	2,411,900
7	Netherlands	446,416	473,473	478,318
8	Spain	834,369	910,928	1,014,077

2 Select Insert, Chart from the menu bar, to start the Chart Wizard or click on the Chart Wizard on the toolbar.

3 The Chart Wizard takes you through four steps to create the chart. Step 1 displays a dialog box with a list of chart types in the left pane, and a preview window on the right.

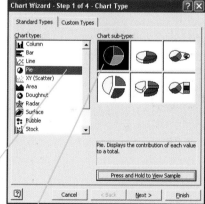

4 Select Pie from the left pane. In the Preview pane, the sample in black is the default choice.

5 Use the Press and Hold facility to view a sample of your data in the chosen chart style.

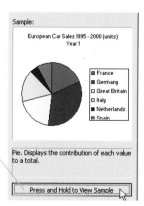

6 Select Next to move to the next step.

Create a pie chart – step 2

1 Step two of the Wizard highlights with a flashing dotted line, the data range you had previously selected.

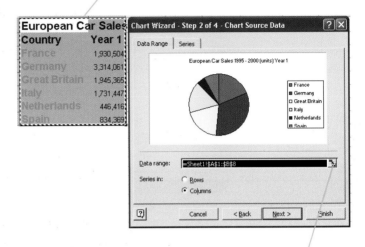

The Collapse Dialog button was used with the Formula Function in Excel. See

page 94.

2 If necessary, reselect the data range. Click on the Collapse dialog button. This reduces this window to just a bar, allowing you to view the selected data range, and change it if necessary. Click again on the button to re-display the window.

The Series tab will be examined in greater detail, later in the unit. See pages

160-161.

3 The Series tab shows where the Wizard is getting the information. It is using Sheet 1, cells B1 and B2 for the specific name, and B3 to B8 for the values.

4 The Category labels, France, Germany etc. are found on Sheet 1, cells A3 to A8. Excel applied the correct labels because the data range was pre-selected.

Create a pie chart – step 3

1 This next step allows you to add the required details to the chart. The Chart title has been created from information on the spreadsheet. You can amend it now if it is not as specified in the exercise.

Note that at any point in the Charting process you can cancel, or go backwards. You can also select Finish, but this does skip two stages that are designed to help with the finer details of the chart.

2 The Wizard has automatically generated a legend. For a pie chart, the legend may not be the best way to identify the different sectors. Select the Legend tab, and remove the tick.

In a coloured pie chart, and specifically with a colour printed pie chart, the legend will identify the various sectors. However, with a black and white print, the differences are not so obvious. See page 162 for how to change the way the sectors are displayed.

3 Select the Data Labels tab and view the effects of selecting the different options offered. The best combination for the CLAIT exercise is the Category name and Percentage or Value. Using the Category name ensures that there is no confusion over sector identity on the finished print.

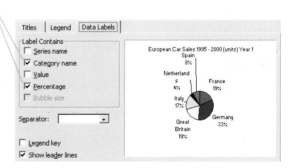

4 The Wizard preview window is very small, so the charts are not well illustrated. The finished chart will correct any apparent presentation problems.

Create a pie chart – step 4

If you don't supply a name for the new sheet, it will be called Chart 1, or Chart 2 etc.

To delete the chart when it is an object on the sheet, select it and press the delete key.

The chart has its own frame, and can be re-sized and moved the same as any picture or image frame. For more on frames see Unit 6, Desktop publishing, or Unit 8, Computer art.

Check your finished graph to ensure that you have not included blank cells. These will show as a thin line and a 0% allocation. Also make sure that any headings or axes entries are spelled correctly.

1 The last step in the Wizard is to select how to view the chart. For the New CLAIT course,

the best presentation is on its own sheet. Supply a name for the chart sheet, to help identify it and click Finish. To review the underlying data, select the Sheet tab. Any changes made to the data will be reflected in the chart.

| European Car Sales 95-2000 | Sheet1 | Sheet2 | Sheet3 |

2 The default on Step 4 is to view the chart as an embedded object in the current sheet, with the data source identified, as shown below.

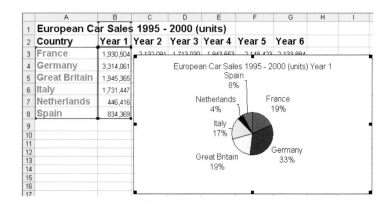

3 To change the chart from its own sheet or as Object in, select Chart, Location. (The chart must be selected to see Chart on the toolbar.) This invokes the dialog box as shown above.

Bar/column chart

The data that you are using for all the graphs is usually one range of consecutive cells. Make sure that you select that part of the range that you want to use, each time you start a new graph.

For the purposes of the New CLAIT course, the bar and column chart formats are equally acceptable. Microsoft prefers to use the term Bar for horizontal columns, and Column for vertical. To create a bar or column chart:

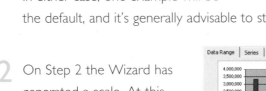

1 Select your data and click on the Chart Wizard. Select Column or Bar. In either case, one example will be the default, and it's generally advisable to stay with the default.

2 On Step 2 the Wizard has generated a scale. At this point you must accept the upper and lower ranges and must wait until the chart is finished. See page 159 for how to change the scale.

The bar or column graph shows a discrete or specific value, usually at a point in time. It is also used for comparing sets of data values.

3 Step 3 allows you to add a title and X and Y axis labels. For this chart you must enter the title as Excel does not do it for you.

As you type into the relevant boxes, the information will be added to the preview.

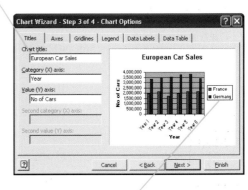

4 This step allows you to modify the position of the legend, or remove it. However, unlike the pie chart, the legend on this graph is essential.

5 Click Next to move to the final step, select a location and Finish.

Line graph

Save each chart as a separate sheet. When you are finished you should have the data on Sheet 1 and several chart sheets.

1 The line graph is created in the same way as the bar and column charts. Select the appropriate data, start the Chart Wizard and follow all the steps.

2 To change the lines on the line graph to make them more significant, select the line itself. Then click with the right mouse button to bring up the Context menu.

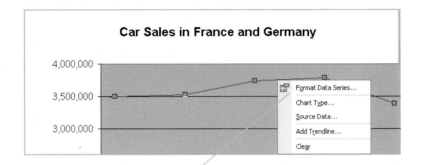

3 Select Format Data Series. This dialog box allows you to change the line colour, style and thickness of the line. You will need to perform this action for each line in the chart.

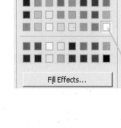

4 To change the grey background, position the mouse in the Plot Area and click with the right mouse button. From the Context menu select Format Plot Area.

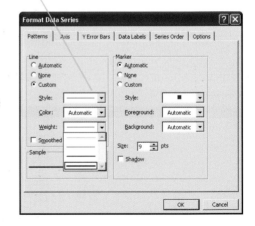

The Plot Area of the Bar and Column charts can be changed in the same way as the Line graph.

5 To change the Plot Area to white, click on the white square and select OK.

Editing charts

Each part of a chart is a separate entity that can be edited, moved and changed independently. When you click to select any part of the chart you will see its frame.

When the Chart sheet is the active sheet, you will see Chart appear on the Menu bar, providing access to the Chart options and functions.

1 To add a chart title or axis labels, click in the chart to activate it, and from the Menu bar select Chart, Chart Options. This displays the window available on Step 3 of the Wizard, see page 153. You can now add or amend the title and labels.

2 To simply amend the title or labels, click on the item twice. The first click selects the item, the second positions the cursor, ready for you to use the normal editing tools.

Car Sales in France and Germany

You can use the Context menu, invoked by the right mouse button, for most of these items.

3 To edit the actual figures that are plotted, return to the original data, and make the amendments there. The plotted graph will automatically change to reflect the new figures.

4 To change the data range that is plotted, select the chart and from the Menu choose Chart, Source data. This displays the dialog box, as shown in Step 2 of the Wizard, see page 152. Use the Collapse dialog button to minimise the window, and reselect the range.

For details on how to change the chart location see page 154.

5 Note that in re-selecting the data range, the legend has changed to identify the lines as Series 1 and 2. See pages 160-161 for how to correct.

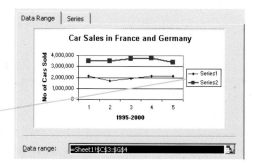

The chart toolbar

The chart toolbar provides some useful facilities, and is a quick way to access some of the most used functions. To view the chart toolbar:

1 Select View, Toolbars, and the Chart toolbar.

2 The toolbar may appear on its own line under the Standard or Formatting toolbar, or it may float on the screen.

Chart Objects list   Format button   Legend toggle   Data table view   Angle text

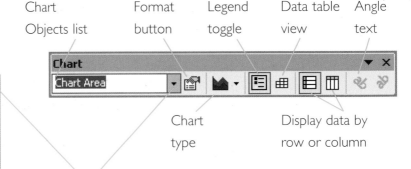

Chart type   Display data by row or column

3 The Chart Objects list displays the name of the part of the chart selected. To format any part, select from the drop-down list and click on the Format button.

4 The Chart type can be changed by selecting from a series of styles displayed on the Chart type button.

5 The Legend and Data table options are both toggle switches, so you can see the chart with and without these additions.

6 You can use the Display data by row or column buttons to view the other way to present the data, if the default does not suit you.

Amend the scale

The Y axis is the value axis, in other words, it shows the number sold, or the cost of sales, or the value of sales. The Y axis on the Bar chart is horizontal, and on the Column chart it is vertical.

The scale measurements are automatically created by Excel, based on the information in the spreadsheet. In the CLAIT exercise you will be required to display the scale with a particular maximum and minimum.

Check that the whole of the chart area is not selected. The selection handles should only appear on the Y axis. When the mouse pointer is on the correct axis, it will display the Value Axis message.

1 Select the Y axis. It should display the selection handles, top and bottom. Stay on the axis and click with the right mouse button to access the Context menu.

2 Select Format Axis, and the Scale tab. The CLAIT exercise will tell you what to set as the minimum and maximum.

3 Check the Major and Minor unit. Problems arise when the difference between the Minimum and Maximum is not divisible by the Major unit. This may change the point at which the axes cross, or cause a different maximum from that specified, to be used.

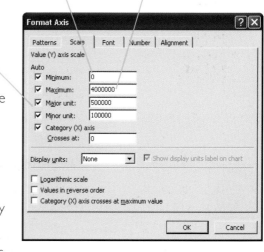

When you change the font size, style or alignment, it only applies to the selected axis. Select the other axis and follow the same procedure.

4 Use this dialog box to change the font size, style and alignment.

The data

The Series tab on Step 2 of the Wizard, see page 152, shows where on the spreadsheet the data has been selected, and how it has been used. For creating a simple pie, bar or line chart, you may never need to look at this tab or make any changes to it. There are, however, some circumstances that may arise during the completion of an exercise where amending these details becomes necessary.

The Legend

You can check the Legend on Step 2 of the Wizard, when you first create the chart, and make these changes then.

You may find that when your chart has been created there is no legend, or the legend entry reads Series 1, and/or 2. So you can interpret the Chart, the legend must specify the correct series names.

1 Select the chart, and from the Menu click Chart, Source Data. Click the Series tab, if necessary.

2 The Wizard has used the cell address in the Name box to find the series name, ie France in A3, and the matching values from the adjacent cells on the spreadsheet, B3 to G3.

3 If the name box is blank or the Series box contains Series 1, click on the Collapse dialog button in the Name box and select the cell on the spreadsheet that contains the appropriate name. You would need to select each series in the list, e.g. Series 2 (Germany) and perform the same actions again.

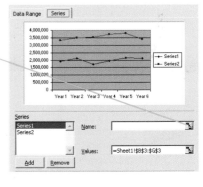

The Legend must clearly identify the different series. If you are printing on a black and white printer, make sure that the differences are discernible. See page 162.

Data labels

There are occasions when the data labels are numbers, such as years, part numbers, ages etc. The Wizard will automatically plot these, creating a series entry for them. In plotting the data labels, the Wizard does not use them to assign an identity to the data.

Notice how in this example the Chart Wizard has taken the Country and year dates as data to be plotted. Also, the X axis data labels are missing, and the default values of 1-5 have been used.

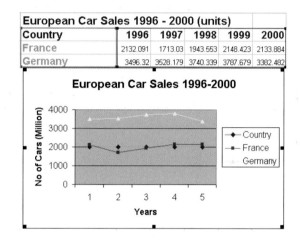

European Car Sales 1996 - 2000 (units)					
Country	1996	1997	1998	1999	2000
France	2132.091	1713.03	1943.553	2148.423	2133.884
Germany	3496.32	3528.179	3740.339	3787.679	3382.482

1 To remove the incorrect series, select Chart, Source Data, and the Series tab.

In Format, Cells, there is an option to treat numbers as text. Unfortunately this just changes the alignment, the Chart Wizard will still plot them as numbers.

2 In the Series pane select the entry that is not required and Remove. You will see the effect immediately in the preview pane.

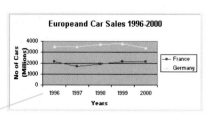

3 These numbers can now be used as the X axis labels. Click the Collapse dialog button to return to the spreadsheet and select them. Again, you should see the effect in the preview pane.

Changing segment display

For a chart to be useable, the data it is illustrating must be clearly identified. Colour monitors make it easy to differentiate between pie chart segments, or lines on a line graph. However, the printed copy may be quite different. Shades of grey or deeper colours may appear very much alike.

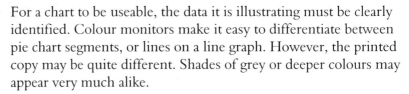

1   To change a segment on a pie chart click on the pie itself, and then click on the particular segment. The first click selects the pie and the second the segment. Still on the segment, right click and select Format Data Point.

2   From the Format Data Point dialog box select the Fill Effects option, and then the Pattern tab.

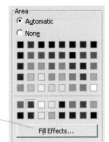

3   Select from the numerous options, remembering to ensure that the final choice clearly identifies the segment.

4   The same process applies to bar and column charts. Select the series you wish to amend. Right click and select Format Data Series.

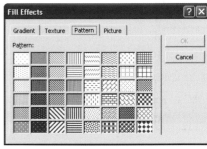

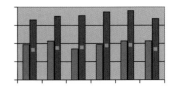
5   The whole series has been selected in this example. If you were to click again on one column, you would select just that one.

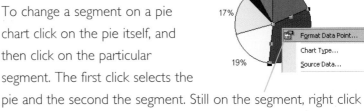

Printing charts

Printing the charts is a very simple process. For New CLAIT it is sufficient to print each chart on a separate page.

1 With the chart on the screen, select Print Preview.

If you don't need to change anything, you can just click on Print.

Next | Previous | Zoom | Print... | Setup... | Margins | Page Break Preview | Close

2 To change the orientation select Setup and the Page tab. Click OK to return to the Preview window. Click Close on the Preview window to return to the Chart.

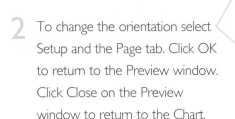

3 The Chart tab provides more printing options, for example to print in black and white. This is a quick way to change the chart to ensure that the segments are noticably different when printed.

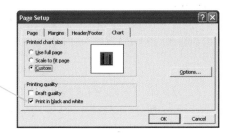

4 To print a reduced size chart, select Custom and OK.

5 You must return to the Chart sheet, not the Preview window, to change the size. Click on the chart to display the selection handles, and drag to resize.

Exercise

Scenario

Your manager has asked you to produce some reports in graph format relating to The Elms Garden Centre.

1. Open the Excel file The Elms.xls, which contains data on sales by various departments for January to June.

It contains the following table:

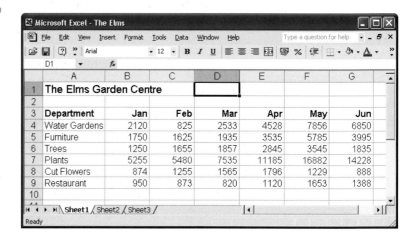

Department	Jan	Feb	Mar	Apr	May	Jun
Water Gardens	2120	825	2533	4528	7856	6850
Furniture	1750	1625	1935	3535	5785	3995
Trees	1250	1655	1857	2845	3545	1835
Plants	5255	5480	7535	11185	16882	14228
Cut Flowers	874	1255	1565	1796	1229	888
Restaurant	950	873	820	1120	1653	1388

The first report will compare sales of each department for the month of January, using a pie chart.

2. Create a pie chart to display the January data for all the departments.

   Give the chart the title Department Sales for January 2002

   Ensure that each sector is shaded or coloured so that the data can be clearly identified when printed.

   Each sector of the chart must be labelled clearly with the department name and either the value or the percentage of sales.

3. Save the file using the name The Elms Sales

4. Print one copy of the pie chart.

The Franchise Manager has asked you to produce a bar chart of the value of sales for the Water Gardens Franchise, over the six month period January to June.

5. Create a bar chart showing the data for Water Gardens from January to June.

   Display the months along the x-axis

   Set the y-axis to display the range 0 to 9000

   Give the chart the title Water Garden Sales

   Give the x-axis the title Month

   Give the y-axis the title Sales

6. Save the file, keeping the name The Elms Sales.

7. Print one copy of the bar chart.

The Centre Manager wants to evaluate sales values for Water Gardens and Furniture and has asked you to produce a line graph comparing their sales over six months.

8. Create a line graph comparing the data for Water Gardens and Furniture for January to June.

   Display the months along the x-axis.

   Set the y-axis range from 1000 to 8000

   Give the graph the tile Comparison of Water Garden and Furniture Sales

   Label the x-axis Month

   Label the y-axis Sales Values

   Use a legend to identify each line. Make sure that the lines and/or data points can be easily identified when printed.

9. Save the file keeping the name The Elms Sales.

10. Print one copy of the line graph.

11. Close the file and exit the software correctly.

Checklist

When you have finished the exercise, use the following checklist. Have you:

- Opened or used the correct file
- Used the correct data range for each chart
- Created the correct type of chart in each case
- Used the specified titles and axes labels, with no spelling errors
- Clearly identified each sector on the pie chart
- Included a legend where required
- Amended the scale where required
- Saved the file using the specified file name
- Printed and closed the file

Answers

Pie Chart

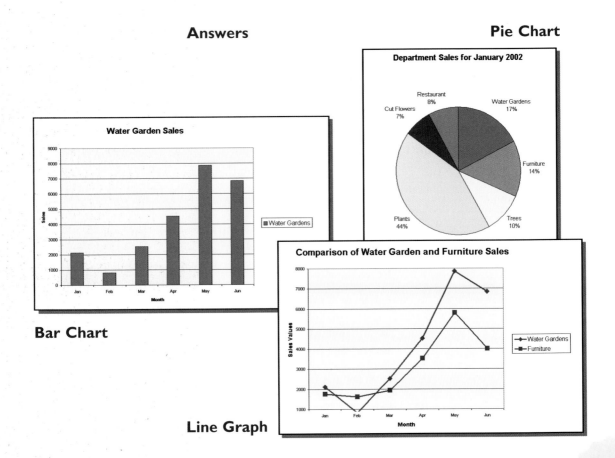

Bar Chart

Line Graph

Computer art

This unit covers the computer art facilities available in
Microsoft Office. It shows how to use vector and bitmapped
images, together with drawing tools to create items of artwork.

Covers

Unit Eight

Computer art

You do not have to be artistic, or good at drawing to attempt this unit.

A colour printer is required for this unit.

Desktop publishing shows how easy it is to create a publication using imported images and text and placing them on the page. The drawing tools, border options, and different fonts sizes and styles means that it is simple to create a professional looking document.

In this unit you are going to create a piece of artwork. In fact, what you are really required to do, is to compose a series of separate items into a specified design. The layout of the artwork is supplied, as are the images that you will need. Sizes, shapes and colours are specified, and to achieve the finished item, you will also use some of the standard drawing tools.

Many of the necessary tools and facilities exist in several of the Office products. Microsoft Visio is the designated drawing program that goes with the Office Suite of programs. Visio is however sold as a separate item and not included in the Office Suite. Although not as comprehensive, Word provides all the facilities and tools needed to complete the New CLAIT exercise.

In creating the artwork for this New CLAIT unit you will be using two different types of graphics, bitmap and vector.

Bitmap images

Bitmap images, also known as raster images, are based on pixels. Each pixel is a tiny block, containing one colour. If you were to zoom in on a bitmap image, you would eventually begin to see the picture breakdown into blocks or become pixelated.

There is a bewildering number of different graphics file formats used. Nearly every software program has its own 'native' file format. Always save your file in this native format before you save it in any other. You may for instance want to save it as a GIF or JPEG to send over the Internet.

The advantage of pixel based images is that each pixel can take a different shade of colour, thus providing depth, shadow and texture to images. Bitmap images are used for photographs and most pictures you will see on the Internet. The images that you will import in the exercise will be bitmap images.

For an in depth tutorial on image formats, and the background to the different types look at the Kodak site at www.kodak.com.

The disadvantage of the bitmap format is that it does not resize well. If you resize a picture, making it larger, the software has to compensate and fill in the gaps. A dithering or antialiasing function is used to smooth out the differences in colour and lines. If you make the picture smaller, then it has to guess which pixels to drop, and so some of the detail gets lost.

The most common bitmap file formats are:

- TIFF   Tag Image File Format
- JPEG   Joint Photographic Experts Group
- GIF   Graphical Interchange Format

Vector images

Vector graphics do not use pixels, instead they describe an image in terms of shapes, lines and text. They are based on mathematical formulae and measurements that represent lines and curves. Because they plot or draw a line between two points they are very smooth and have the great advantage that they can be scaled or resized. Vector graphics are particularly suited to geometric shapes, and will be used in this unit to draw lines and circles.

Vector graphics use gradations of colour, but it is more difficult to create shading. They cannot represent irregular details and fine changes of texture or tint and are totally impossible for the level of detail, such as found in photographs.

The most common vector file formats are:

- WMF   Windows Metafile
- AI   Adobe Illustrator
- EPS   Encapsulated Postscript

When you view an image on the screen, you are probably seeing it at 90 pixels to the square inch. When you print it, your printer may achieve 300-600 dots per inch. What looks good on the screen, may not look so good printed, as the software has to fill in the extra dots.

1   This first Alphabet is a scaled bitmap representation and shows the stepped effect of a pixelated image.

2   The second example shows the same image with antialiasing applied. The grey pixels help smooth the stepping.

Alphabet

Alphabet

3   With vectors, images can be enlarged indefinitely without loss of shape.

Alphabet

The canvas

Word creates a canvas to hold your artwork. This provides a working area that must be selected when you use the drawing tools or insert images.

1 Open Word. You will be working in the Print layout view. If you are using a different view, Word will automatically switch views as you create the drawing canvas.

Working with a canvas allows you to move all the objects on the canvas together, if, for example, you wanted to insert it into the middle of a text area.

2 Select Insert, Picture, New Drawing. Word places a Drawing Canvas on the blank page. The rectangle appears within the margins, at a default size.

3 You should also see the Drawing Canvas toolbar, only available when the canvas is selected.

Note that Word uses the Print Layout view.

Create your drawing here.

If the Drawing tools do not appear automatically, select View, Toolbars, Drawing or click on the Drawing button:

4 The Drawing toolbar will appear at the bottom of the window, if not already present.

The Drawing tools

The Drawing tools are available in several of the Office programs.

HOT TIP

Tool tips are the descriptive text that appears when you move the mouse over a button. To make them appear, select View, Toolbars, Customise. On the Options tab, select Show ScreenTips on toolbars.

1 The Draw button provides a popup menu which includes the positioning and alignment facilties. Click on the arrow to view the menu.

2 Autoshapes provides a variety of different and interesting shapes, quite fun to experiment with and use.

3 Simple lines, arrows, rectangles and circles are used frequently, so appear on the toolbar itself. These, and the Autoshapes are vector graphics.

HOT TIP

The Status bar below the Drawing tools indicates how to use the selected tools.

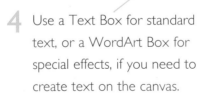

HOT TIP

Select Tools, Options and the General tab. Check that the box to Automatically create drawing canvas is selected.

4 Use a Text Box for standard text, or a WordArt Box for special effects, if you need to create text on the canvas.

5 The colouring tools and line styles apply to frames, text and shapes, created by the other tools.

BEWARE

If you have a canvas but it is not selected, Word will create another one. Be careful that you do not create lots of canvases!

6 To insert an image file, select the ClipArt or Image from file tools.

7 Click on a tool to create an object. If you do not already have a canvas, one will be created for you.

Set the artwork size

You would expect to be able to specify a canvas size at the beginning and rely on it maintaining that size throughout its use. However, Word resizes the canvas when you draw larger shapes or import larger items. To set a fixed dimension to your working area, you must draw a rectangle within the canvas and set the size of the rectangle to the finished dimensions of the artwork.

1 Make sure that the Drawing canvas is selected. Click on the Rectangle drawing tool and move the mouse to the canvas. The mouse pointer becomes crosshairs.

2 Press the left mouse button and drag diagonally down and draw a box. You do not need to draw the exact shape required.

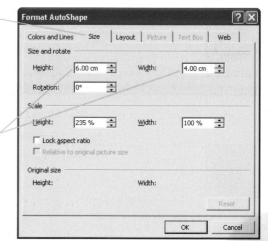

The Rectangle Autoshape has a border of a thin line. This can be widened or removed. See page 179.

3 With the box still selected, click the right mouse button and select Format Autoshape.

4 Select the Size tab from the Format Autoshape dialog box.

5 Set the Height and Width of the shape to be the finished size of the artwork. Then click OK.

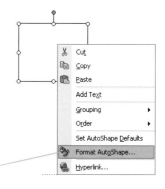

Insert an image

You will be given the images that you need to use. To insert the image:

You will usually have a choice of image, a GIF and a JPEG. Both are acceptable formats for using in Word. The GIF file will usually be a larger data size, even though the images look the same.

1 The canvas area should be selected, or the picture will arrive elsewhere in the document, even on a separate page if it is large.

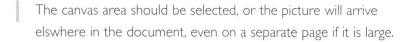

2 Select Insert, Picture, From File, or click on the button. The default folder for images is My Pictures. You may need to browse through the folders to find the file. Select the Thumbnails view of the folder contents to help in finding the correct file.

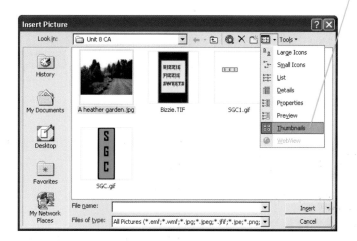

The Picture toolbar should appear. It may float on the window as shown, or appear as a separate toolbar under the Standard toolbar. You can drag and drop it onto the Standard or Formatting toolbar if you wish to anchor it.

3 Select the required file and click on Insert. The image appears on the canvas, with sizing and rotation handles.

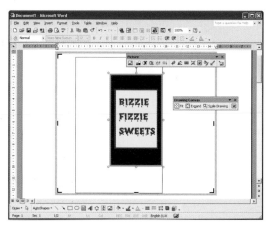

Manage the image

Resize

The image has resize handles located at the corners and the middle of the sides. However, to resize the image, you should only use the corner handles, as these will maintain the correct proportions of the picture. If you need to set the image to a specific dimension, use the Format Picture facility.

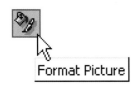

Format Picture

1 With the image selected, right click and select Format Picture, or click on the Format Picture button. Select the Size tab and specify the height **OR** width but not both.

2 The Scale will alter automatically as you change one of the dimensions. The Lock aspect ratio box should be ticked to ensure that the image maintains the correct proportions.

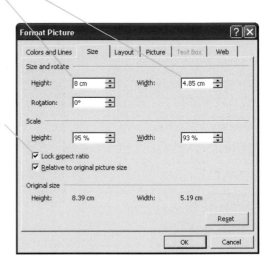

Rotate

You can use the Rotation option in this window to specify an exact number of degrees. A plus figure will rotate the image to the right, or clockwise. The button on the Picture toolbar will rotate the image to the left. You would have to rotate the image through 270 degrees, or three clicks to achieve the same effect.

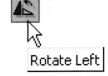

Rotate Left

The image file on disk remains as it was originally. It is only the area that is displayed that has been cropped.

Crop

To crop an image means to remove part of the picture.

Crop

1 Select the image you wish to crop. Click on the Crop tool on the Picture toolbar. Initially the mouse is shown with the Crop tool attached. The image itself will have the cropping handles shown, not the select handles.

2 As you move onto the canvas area, the mouse changes to a normal arrow. In the image area it becomes a fourheaded arrow, the move symbol.

3 When you position the mouse over the cropping handles, it changes shape again. In the corner it is a corner, on the end or side it is shown as a T-shape.

To crop on both sides at the same time, press Ctrl as you drag the middle handle. To crop on all four sides, press Ctrl as you drag the corner handle.

4 Select the handle on the side you wish to remove, press the mouse button and drag. When you have finished, you must deselect the Crop tool.

Flip

If you are using an older version of Word, you will need to cut or copy and paste the image into Paint to flip or rotate it. It can then be copied and pasted back into Word.

5 The Flip facility is accessed from the Draw menu on the Drawing toolbar. Select the image and flip as required. This image has been flipped horizontally.

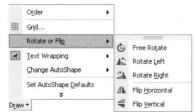

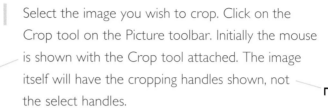

Position the image

If an image is required to fit edge to edge, then select the Format Picture button and specify the size to be the same as the defining rectangle. Make sure that the Lock aspect ratio box is ticked to prevent image distortion. See page 174.

1   Drag the images and place them within the rectangle that you created and sized for the artwork. Most images will only need to be placed in an approximate position.

2   To postion the image exactly, you must make the canvas and the rectangle the same size. This allows you to specify the object's position in the drawing canvas.

3   Shrink the canvas by clicking on the Fit button. Note that you must have at least two objects on the canvas for the Fit button to be enabled. The canvas will wrap to the size of the rectangle.

4   Select the Format Picture button, and the Layout tab. Specify a postion within the canvas, using the top left corner as the reference and click on OK.

Underlying the canvas is a hidden grid which influences the placement of images. You may be aware that as you try to position objects, they shift slightly. The objects are 'snapping to the grid'. This can cause problems with positioning an image or object exactly where you want. To override the Grid, hold down the Alt key as you drag and place an object.

5   The Draw menu provides a Nudge facility, but it is much simpler to use the keyboard. Hold down the Ctrl key and press the arrow key for the direction you wish to move the object. The object moves 0.02 of a cm for every key stroke, and makes it much easier to position objects close to the edges.

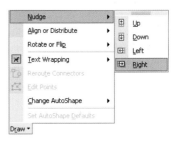

Text boxes

Text on the canvas is created within a text box.

1   Select the Text box tool, move the mouse to
    the working rectangle and draw a box.

2   The normal typing and editing tools apply. On the Formatting
    toolbar, the Bold, Italic and Underline buttons are available, and

the alignment tools. To centre the text on the artwork, first
centre the Text box, and
then click the Centre button
to centre the text within.

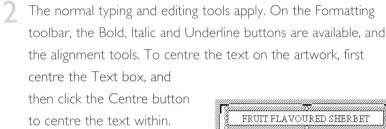

*To delete a Text
Box select the
edge of the box
and press delete.*

3   Dragging a handle of the Text box will
    reshape the box and the text will re-flow
    automatically to fit. It will also maintain its
    alignment attributes.

4   Select the text style from the Formatting toolbar; all the Word text
    styles are available. For the size, you must select appropriately. To get
    the best font size, first select the text. Hold down the Ctrl key and
    press [(the open square bracket) to increase the font size one point
    at a time, or] (close square
    bracket) to decrease
    one point at a time.

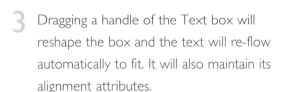

5   The Format Text Box menu
    entry only appears if you right
    click on the edge of the Text
    box. If you are in the Text box
    itself, the text options apply.

AutoShapes

You will be required to make a shape, such as a square or circle and reproduce it several times. Make the first one, and then select Copy and then Paste. You can continue to Paste until you have sufficient. You can select and position each one independently.

The Autoshapes menu provides a wide variety of shapes. You can select from the Autoshapes menu on the Drawing Toolbar, see page 171, or you can choose Insert, Picture, Autoshapes. The Autoshapes toolbar will appear and float over the page. The Autoshapes toolbar allows you to select from a category of shapes. If you are going to select from that category several times, you can get the subset toolbar to also float.

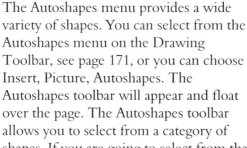

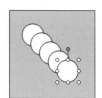

1   With the standard shapes of lines, ovals and rectangles, click on the tool once to use it once.

   Double click the tool to use it multiple times. De-select it when finished. For the more elaborate shapes, you must select each time.

2   To draw a straight horizontal, vertical or diagonal line, hold down the Shift key as you drag the mouse. To reposition the line, first select it so the selection handles appear. You can then drag it. To resize it, positon the cursor on one of the selection handles and drag in the required direction, holding down the Shift key if necessary.

To draw a perfect circle, select the Oval and hold down the Shift key as you draw.

3   Any of the Autoshapes will maintain perfect proportions if you hold down the Shift key as you draw. For example, to draw a square select the Rectangle tool and hold down the Shift key as you draw.

4   To position any of the Autoshapes exactly you can hold down the Alt key as you drag and place it. See the Hot Tip at the bottom of page 176.

Borders and lines

If the image has an outlining box as part of the image, you can only remove it by using the Crop facility.

Text boxes have a narrow black outline by default. Many images have no outline, but have a background colour that delineates the perimeter. You can choose a line style, or to have no line.

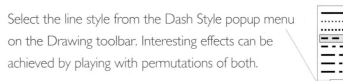

1 The Line Style tools apply to whichever object is selected, Autoshapes, lines, images or text boxes. Select the object.

2 Choose the thickness from the Line Style popup menu on the Drawing toolbar.

3 Select the line style from the Dash Style popup menu on the Drawing toolbar. Interesting effects can be achieved by playing with permutations of both.

4 In some of the CLAIT exercises you may need to remove the outline of an object. Select the object and click on the Format Text, or Format Autoshape or Picture button. You may also select More Styles from the Line Style menu.

See page 181 for more information on text appearing to float over the background.

5 Use the Colour and Lines tab to access the Line Color option and select No Line. You can use the options here to specify a particular line weight and style. Note, as No Line is selected, the Style and Weight options are not available.

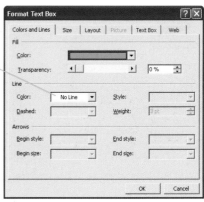

Colouring tools

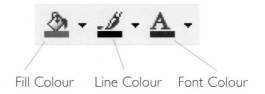

Fill Colour Line Colour Font Colour

1 Each of the colouring tools apears on the Drawing toolbar, and shows the most recently used colour. Click on the arrow next to each tool to view and select from the standard range of colours. If you have Tool Tips switched on, the colour name will be shown.

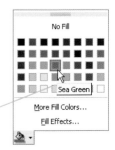

2 The Fill Colour tool works with Autoshapes and Text boxes. Select the object to fill and then select the colour. To leave the background white, use No Fill.

3 In the example shown here, the rectangle used to delineate the artwork size has been filled. Note that the Text Box, image and Autoshape have remained white.

4 Select Fill Effects to add Gradient, Texture, Pattern or a Picture to the object. You can change the colour selected, set a Transparency level, or change the angle of the shading.

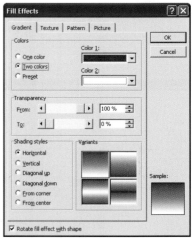

5   The Line colour works with Autoshapes and the borders of images and Text boxes. The default line colour is black. To change the colour, select the object and click on the new colour.

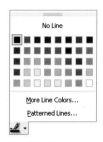

6   Select Patterned Lines to see more options. Interesting effects can be achieved by changing the Foreground and Background colours.

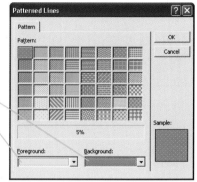

7   To colour the text , select the text itself and then the colour.

8   In some examples of artwork the text appears to float over the background with no outline. To achieve this effect, select the Text box, and then choose No Line from the toolbar, and Fill with the same colour as the background.

FRUIT FLAVOURED SHERBET

You must select a Fill colour. If No Fill is selected, the Transparency option is not available.

9   Alternatively, select Format Text Box, see page 177. Select any colour for Fill and set the Transparency level to 100%. You must also select No Line.

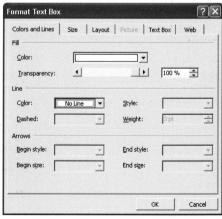

WordArt

The WordArt Gallery is available in Word, Excel, Publisher, FrontPage and PowerPoint.

Type your text on three lines in the Edit WordArt Text window to display it with this shape.

Click on the WordArt button on the Drawing toolbar to open the WordArt Gallery.

1. The WordArt Gallery previews 30 different styles of WordArt. Those illustrated are only the starting point. All the effects of colour, shape and outline can be altered.

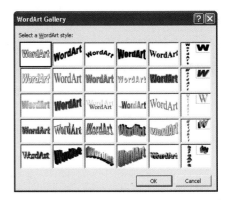

2. Select the style and click OK. You will be shown the Edit WordArt Text window. Do as instructed to type your text and click OK. Note that the Font style and size are pre-selected. You can change them if you wish.

3. Your text will be placed on the page with selection handles. WordArt has the same options as other Text Boxes and objects.

4. The selection handles allow you to re-size the text box and also to increase or decrease the curvature. Select a corner and drag. You will see a projected new shape as you drag.

WordArt Toolbar

The WordArt toolbar provides easy access if you wish to make any amendments.

Insert WordArt   Gallery   Shape   Letter height   Alignment

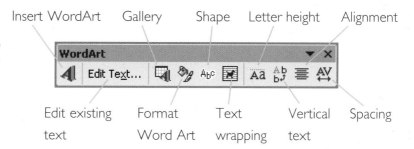

Edit existing text   Format Word Art   Text wrapping   Vertical text   Spacing

Wrapping options are not available if the WordArt is on the Drawing canvas. The Layout tab in Format WordArt offers positional measurements.

5 To change the colour, right click on the edge of the WordArt box and select Format WordArt. Use this window to specify both the Fill Colour and the outline colour and weight.

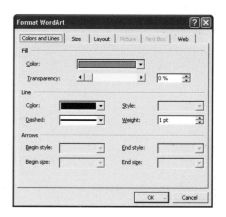

6 To move and position WordArt select the Layout tab, the default is to place the object In line with text. Select Advanced and Through to be able to float the WordArt on the page.

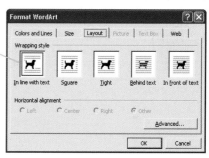

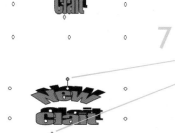

7 The WordArt text will display the green Rotation handle and the yellow Reshaping handle. Drag the reshaping handle to vary the proportions.

Layers

You may only need to adjust the 3D position when you have to make final changes to the artwork.

Each object that you place on the canvas has a horizontal and vertical position. As you build the artwork in layers, each object gets superimposed over the previous one, so they also have a third dimensional position. If the objects do not overlap, this is not obvious. However, if they do overlap then one or other may be partially or fully obscured. To understand the layering effect:

1 Click on an object and drag and drop it over part of another object so one partly obscures the other.

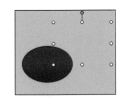

2 Select the uppermost object and click Draw, Order and choose Send Backward.

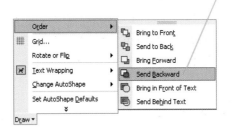

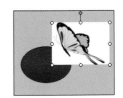

If you click on the object with just the handles remaining, it will disappear altogether! See Step 4.

3 If you select Send to Back, you will only see the object's handles. To view it again, select Bring to Front.

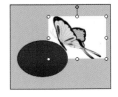

4 For the CLAIT exercise, the first object created was the defining rectangle. If any objects that have been placed on it have disappeared, select it and use the Send to Back option.

5 You can also position objects in front or behind regular Word text.

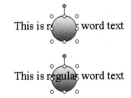

Canvas management

For the CLAIT exercise you only need to print the canvas. There is no requirement to print text at the side.

1 Throughout this unit you have used a Drawing canvas. For the CLAIT exercise the canvas has its limitations as its size cannot be locked. However it does allow you to move the objects together, maintaining their relative positions and size.

2 The default layout for the canvas is In line with text. If you wish to use it with text, select the text wrapping button. Choose the most appropriate from the available options.

When you are positioning the canvas, it is a good idea to change the screen zoom level to Whole Page or Two Pages, as the canvas does jump around.

3 You are now able to drag and position the canvas in the middle of text. Make sure that you have the canvas edge, and not the background rectangle edge, when you drag. You will see the outline of all the objects moving together.

4 When you save the artwork, it will be saved as a Word file with the .doc file extension, using the standard Word file management tools.

5 For the CLAIT exercise you will need to print in colour. For details on saving and printing in Word, see pages 39–42.

There is more information on colour printing in Unit 6 Desktop publishing.

Exercise

Scenario

You have been contracted by Surprise Gardens to create a front cover for their gift voucher scheme. The publicity manager has provided a layout of his preferred design.

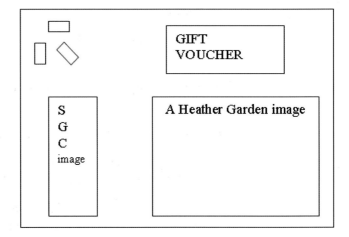

1. Create a new piece of artwork and set the size to be 11 cms high and 15 cms wide. Fill the background with light green.

2. Insert the image Heather Garden and make the following changes:

   Crop the picture to remove most of the bush on the left
   Resize the image, keeping the proportions.
   Flip the image so that the heather bed is on the right
   Position the image at the bottom right of the artwork, as shown in the draft.

3. Above the image, create a box and insert the following text, in dark blue:
   GIFT VOUCHER
   Make the text appear on two lines as shown.

4. Put a wide yellow box around the 'gift voucher' text.

5. Draw an oblong shape and place it in the top left corner. Copy the shape twice and rotate one to a 90 degree angle, and one to a 45 degree angle.

The SGC image file is also in the Unit 8 CA folder.

6. Fill one rectangle with blue, one with yellow and one with red.

7. Import the image file SGC and place it at the bottom left.

8. Resize the image, so that it is 7.00cms tall, keeping the proportions.

9. Save the file using the name Garden Voucher and print one copy.

The Publicity manager has asked you to make the following changes:

10. Delete the diagonal and vertical rectangles.

11. Change the text from GIFT VOUCHER to GARDEN CENTRE GIFT VOUCHER.

12. Resize the text box so that it fits across the top of the artwork, from edge to edge, and the text occupies one line. Centre the text.

13. Remove the yellow border around the text.

14. Fill the text box with the same colour used for the rest of the artwork.

15. Save the file as SCG Voucher and print one copy.

16. Close the file and exit the software.

Checklist

When you have finished the exercise, use the following checklist. Have you:

- Set the correct artwork size and checked the printouts to ensure the required size was maintained
- Imported the correct images
- Positioned and sized them as required
- Created the text as required with no spelling errors
- Created and copied shapes as specified
- Created borders where required
- Used primary and secondary colours only
- Printed the artwork in full colour
- Saved and closed the file and application

Answers

Gift Voucher

Web pages

This unit uses FrontPage to develop a small Web site. It includes importing, creating and formatting Web pages and creating links. It develops an understanding of basic HTML concepts, web page navigation, and browsing.

Covers

Unit Nine

HTML Editors and Browsers

This unit provides you with the knowledge and understanding required to link existing Web pages to a new Web page to form a small Web site. Web pages are defined using HTML (hypertext mark-up language). To create or modify pages, you need a text editor and to display the pages you need a browser.

HTML Text Editor

The HTML Editor displays pages as you see them at the Web site, with effects applied and images displayed and located in their proper positions. This is called WYSIWYG – What You See Is What You Get.

There are several types of text editors that you could use. FrontPage or Dreamweaver, for example, are full function HTML editors. They will generate HTML code for you, and allow you to view the HTML statements in their raw form, or in the final format as they display at the Web site. With these programs you can import and place text and image files, align the page items, adjust font sizes, styles and colours and format the Web page. They also help you to insert links within the page or to other pages. These applications also provide additional facilities to automate the process of creating and maintaining the Web site.

FrontPage also supports the use of XML (extensible markup language) which defines the structure of the data content of a Web page. However, this is not a requirement for the CLAIT exercises.

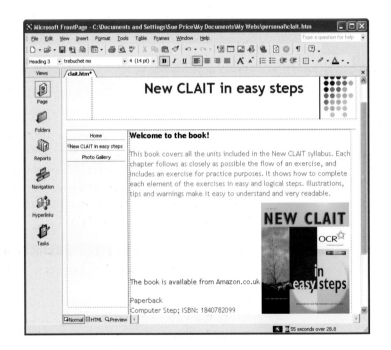

You could use a word processor such as Word or a desktop publishing application such as Publisher that can display and save files in the HTML format. These will provide the WYSIWYG view, and help generate valid HTML statements, but they do not support all the additional functions offered by the HTML editors.

As the HTML file format is plain text, you could use a plain text editor such as NotePad to create and modify the statements, but you would have to understand the HTML format completely. With plain text editors there would be no facilities for displaying text effects or images, or presenting them in the WYSIWYG view. There is also no means for validating the HTML statements. Plain text editors are used by experienced programmers who require full control over the way the HTML code is developed.

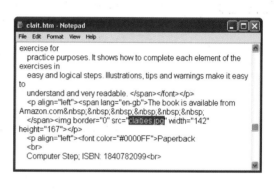

For the purposes of this unit we will be using FrontPage to create, and modify the Web site.

Using a browser to visit Web sites, display Web pages and navigate between Web pages is covered in Unit 3: Electronic Communication, pages 53.

Web Page Browser

You need a Web Browser such as Internet Explorer or Netscape to view, in their final form, the Web pages that you have created. You should do this on your PC, before you send the HTML files to the Web server that supports your Web site. You and your Web site visitors will also use a Web Browser to view and navigate between Web pages at the Web site.

See page 206 for choosing a Web browser to view your Web site in FrontPage.

For the purposes of this unit, we will be using Microsoft Internet Explorer to display and link between Web pages.

Publishing the Web

The final step in creating a Web site is to publish the Web for all to see. You normally use an Internet Service Provider (ISP) who will provide the storage space and host the Web site for you. Publishing is transferring the files from your PC to the Web server. See page 209 for more information.

FrontPage

FrontPage allows you to create Web pages and build Web sites with all the functions and features of a professional Web site. You can use the built-in functions, styles and themes to control the appearance, to save you handling the fine details, but you can also do things for yourself using specific HTML statements where necessary. When you have created the components of your Web site, FrontPage helps you to set it up on a server, manage and monitor its use, and apply updates and changes.

If the Views Bar does not appear, select it from the View menu:

FrontPage views

The Views bar at the side of the FrontPage window lets you switch quickly between the different ways of looking at your Web site contents.

Page view is used for creating and editing Web pages. It lets you see them in the WYSIWYG format, as they would appear in a Web browser. It lets you switch between Normal, HTML and Preview mode.

Folders view shows how the Web content is organised, in the same style of view as Windows Explorer. You can manage the files and folders in this view.

Reports view lets you analyse the contents of your Web. You can determine which files are not linked or out of date, you can calculate the total size of the files, and you can group the files.

Navigation view can be used to create, display and change the navigation structure of the Web. It includes a folder side-bar, from which you can drag and drop pages into your structure.

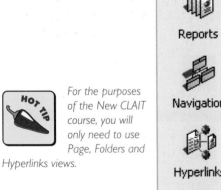

For the purposes of the New CLAIT course, you will only need to use Page, Folders and Hyperlinks views.

Hyperlinks view shows the hyperlinks in your Web, both internal and external. It shows graphically which links are working and which are broken.

Tasks view keeps a record of those tasks that are required to complete or maintain the Website.

From the Windows Desktop select Start, All Programs, Microsoft FrontPage. The first time you open FrontPage, you may be presented with a blank page with the tab title New_Page_1.htm. This is just a default blank page. FrontPage may also open with just toolbars and the Views bar showing.

> Microsoft FrontPage - C:\Documents and Settings\Sue Price\My Documents\My Webs\new_page_1.htm

The FrontPage title bar indicates a complex folder structure. FrontPage will remember any previous Web folders you have created, and will open in the most recently used folder.

> Microsoft FrontPage - C:\Documents and Settings\Sue Price\My Documents\My Webs\personal\clait.htm

For New CLAIT you will be provided with two Web pages, a text file and an image file, with which to create a Web site. These files should be contained within a folder.

Your Web site

A Web site is known as a Web in FrontPage. It is comprised of a Home page, and optionally some secondary pages, each containing text, images and links. The links may be within the page or to other Web pages and Web sites.

To create the Web site, you first create a Web site folder structure. FrontPage does this for you. You then import the existing pages and images. As a third step, you will insert a text and image file, and format the new page to conform with the 'house' style.

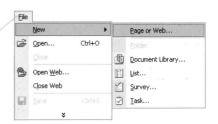

To create a new Web site, select File, New, Page or Web.

Notice how the mouse pointer becomes a hand when over a link to a function in FrontPage.

This displays the Task Pane, where you select Empty Web. An empty Web is a folder that contains a standard set of subfolders.

Build the Web

1 The Empty Web template creates a new Web folder with empty subfolders. The Web folder will be saved into My Documents\My Webs.

The location of the new Web is displayed in a very small window. It is not easy to see the full folder hierarchy. By default, FrontPage remembers the previously used Web name and adds the next consecutive number. It's best to specify a completely new folder name.

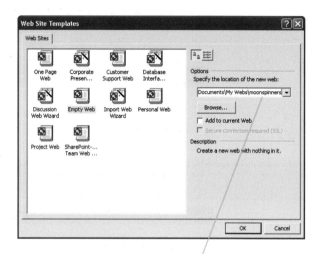

2 Check, and modify if necessary, the full location of the new Web and click on OK. In Explorer view, the Web folder shows the Web symbol. It contains standard folders, two of which are used

moonspinners

The two users folders are not needed in the CLAIT exercises. If you were creating a large Web site, you should use them.

by FrontPage – they are shown in a lighter colour and are normally hidden. The two user folders are Private and Images.

...cont'd

You have been supplied with two Web pages. To use them in the new Web, you must first import them.

Import pages

1 Select File, Import. The Import window will be empty, so click on Add File.

2 You will need to browse through the drive and folder structure to locate the files to add. To select all the files, click on the first and press and hold Shift as you click on the last. Then select Open.

By selecting all the files, you are sure that the associated image files are included in the Web site and can be displayed where required in the Web pages.

3 Select any files not required and click Remove. Click OK to proceed.

4 The files are added to the Web site. Change to the Folder view to see them.

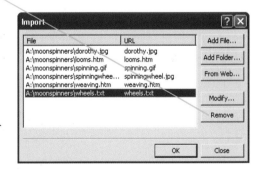

Note how the imported files have been added to the main Web folder, not into the available subfolders.

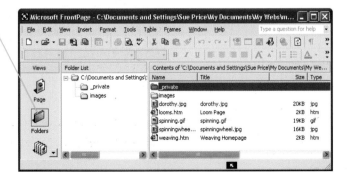

Open Web pages

The Web pages and associated images have been imported into the Web site. To edit and amend the pages you must open them.

Each Web page is a separate file. You can have just one page open, or all the pages open, but you have to open them individually as FrontPage does not allow you to open several files in one action.

1 Select File, Open or click on the Open button. FrontPage switches automatically to the Page view. Check to make sure that you are looking in the correct folder. Open all the necessary files.

You can work with each page independently, but for some operations such as applying formats, it is easier to have them all open at the same time.

2 In Page view you will see each page with a separate tab, giving the file name. Each page also has its own Close button.

If you did not import the image, you will see a place holder on the Web page. To import images see page 195.

3 Page view offers three ways to view each page. Normal view gives a WYSIWYG editing view. It allows normal word processing so you can add and amend text. You can apply format and layout changes and you can create Hyperlinks.

4 HTML view shows the underlying programming code in plain text form, so that you can see exactly what effects and actions have been defined.

The View selected is specific to each page.

5 Preview mode shows the page as it will appear in the browser. Animated effects are enabled and hyperlinks become live.

Create links

The home page is often given a standard name, such as Index.htm or Default.htm. For the purposes of New CLAIT, a meaningful name is used.

A Web page is neither a page nor a screen – it is really just a file that can be viewed on the monitor. Depending on your monitor's resolution and the size of the page, you may see it all at once, or you may have to scroll sideways or down to see it all. You can create links to connect between pages, or between different locations on the same page. To create a link:

1 Highlight the text to use as a link. Select Insert, Hyperlink or click on the button to Insert Hyperlink

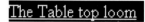

2 The Insert Hyperlink window shows the text used for the link. It is set to link to an existing file or Web page, and is displaying the list of files in the current folder.

If you select the page to link, you will not get any typing errors that prevent the links from working.

Click here to place the link in the current document.

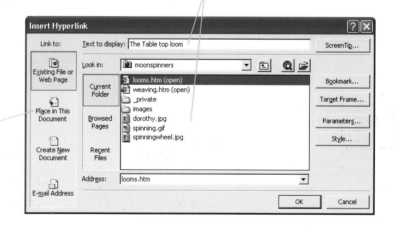

3 Select the page you wish to be linked and click OK. The linked text will be underlined and the mouse changes to a hand when on it. The page does not need to be open for the link to be created. To check the link, press Ctrl while you click, and the linked page will open. Use this method to check links before you save the page.

While the link text is still highlighted, switch to the HTML view to see the link code. The text is highlighted in both views.

`<p><a href="looms.htm">The Table top loom</a></p>`

The Table top loom

Save, Close, Reopen

1 Each Web page can be saved separately. Click on the Save button, or select File, Save. If you have several pages open, select File, Save All. You do not need to save the Web, as such, as the Web is the folder that contains the pages.

2 You can close individual pages, or the whole Web. You will be prompted to save any pages or images that have not been saved previously. You should close one Web before you open another.

The Open button in FrontPage allows you to select file or Web. The button remembers your last action and displays that icon.

3 FrontPage remembers your last status. If you exited with a Web open, it returns to that point. If you closed the Web before you closed FrontPage, it will open with a blank new page.

If your next step is to create a new Web, close the existing Web before you close FrontPage. Otherwise you may find that you have nested your new Web folder within an existing one. See page 194.

4 To reopen a Web page, you can select from Recent Files. This opens the file and containing Web folder. You can select from Recent Webs to open the Web without any pages.

If you have the Task Pane open, you can select an existing file or Web from there.

5 You can also use the Folder view to open Web pages.

Create a new Web page

The CLAIT exercise provides you with a text file, as well as the two Web pages. You will use the text file to populate the new page.

1 With the existing Web pages open, select New Page. It will be inserted as the next page, the tab showing the new_page_htm title.

2 To insert the text file data, select Insert, File. FrontPage opens the My Documents folder. The file should be located in the same folder as the existing Web pages. You will need to navigate the folder structure to locate it.

Remember to save the page when you have inserted the text. You will be prompted for a file name.

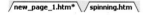

The page tab will change to the new file name.

3 When you open the correct folder, the file may not be visible. You will need to change the Files of type window to look for Text Files. Select the file and click Open.

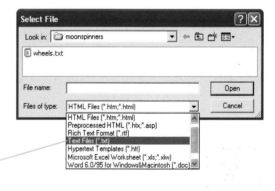

Try other conversion options when you insert the text to see the effect. Remember, you can always click Undo.

4 You will be asked to select a conversion option. The default is Formatted paragraphs. For the text style in most CLAIT exercises, the best option is Normal paragraphs.

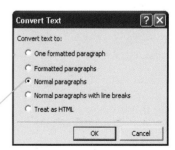

5 Click on OK and the text will be inserted as separate paragraphs.

Format the page

See Unit 10 Presentation Graphics, for more details on house styles.

Most professional publications and presentations have a house style. A hierarchy of page heading, sub heading and paragraph or body text style will be chosen. Page headings will be formatted to a certain font size and style, subheadings to another, and body text to yet another. The two Web pages that were supplied exhibit a house style. The new page must be formatted to conform.

The asterisk next to the tab heading indicates that the page has changed. When you close the Web you will be prompted to save this file.

1 Click on the main heading of the home page. The formatting toolbar will display the style, font name and font size.

Moonspinners Weaving

In this setup, Heading 1 is set as Times New Roman font, 6 (24pt) and bold. FrontPage uses HTML styles rather than standard Office styles.

It also indicates associated formatting such as bold, and alignment.

2 To apply Heading 1 format to the title of the new page, switch to the new page and position the cursor in the title text. You will see that the Style box indicates the current text is Normal.

3 Click the down arrow, and select Heading 1 to apply the new format.

You can use the Format Painter to copy the style from one page to another. Click on the text with the style to copy, select the Format brush and click on the new text to apply the format.

Moonspinners Spinning Equipment

4 Repeat the same procedure to apply the subheading and body text formats to the new page. Select the secondary heading or body text from the home page to confirm the format style, before you apply it to the new page.

5 Line spacing is controlled as in normal word processing.

6 The standard alignment tools work with text and images. Centred items will remain centred on the display, even if you change the screen resolution or the window size.

7 To change the background colour of the current page, select Format, Background. Notice the small Fill button on the command.

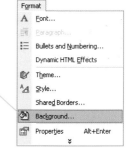

8 Select the Background colour. You may wish to select from More Colours.

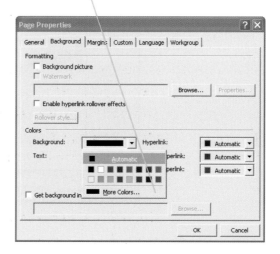

9 FrontPage provides Themes to help you use effective and consistent colouring and layout on your Web. The Theme can be applied to all or selected pages.

Insert an image

Position the cursor where you want to place the picture and select Insert, Picture, From File.

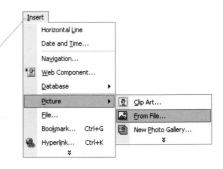

When you import an image or .htm file, a copy is added to your Web and the original stays in the source folder.

FrontPage remembers any previous folder used for image files, so you may need to browse the folders to find the correct one. To help you select the image, select Views from the Picture window and pick Preview. Choose the file and click Insert.

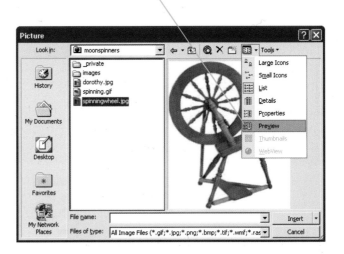

You will be prompted to save any embedded image files, when you save the page.

The default Wrapping style is None. It can remain this way if there is no text on either side.

The image will appear at the cursor position. To enable the correct positioning within the text, you may need to change the image properties. Right click the picture and select Picture Properties.

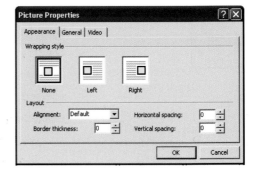

Insert external links

A standard CLAIT exercise requires external links to a Web page, and an e-mail address.

1 The link to the external Web page uses the same mechanism as a link to an internal Web page. Select the text to be linked. Click Insert Hyperlink. See page 197.

2 The external URL address must be typed in to the Address bar. FrontPage inserts the http:// as you type www. Click OK.

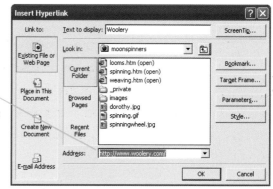

You can open someone else's Web page in FrontPage using this method. You could then adapt it for your own purposes.

3 When you use Ctrl and click to test the link, the Web site will open in FrontPage, with the tab heading [Default Page].

When you have checked a link, you should close the Web page using its Close button. Using the Title bar Close button closes FrontPage altogether.

4 To insert a link to an e-mail address, select the text and Insert Hyperlink. The selected text is placed in the Text to display box. Select the E-mail Address button. When you type the e-mail address FrontPage inserts 'mailto:'. Click OK to complete the process. Note, you cannot check this link using Ctrl and click.

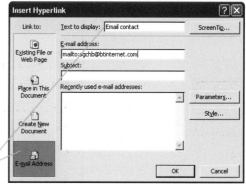

When you click the e-mail link in Preview or browser, it launches your default e-mail program.

Check the links

When you check the links in Preview, the linked page opens on the same page tab, which may cause confusion. Switch back to Normal view to see the pages on their correct page tab.

1 You can check the hypertext links by using Ctrl and click, as shown on page 197. This method is used in Normal page view. It is a quick way to verify most links as you create them, but cannot be used for e-mail links.

| ⬚Normal | ⊞HTML | 🔍Preview |

2 When you have created several links, and saved the pages, check them using the Preview facility. Select the button at the bottom of the screen. You are still running FrontPage, but are using some of the code from Internet Explorer. The advantage is that you are able to view any animated images, and the links are live.

3 Click any link and it loads the linked page onto the same page tab. To check external links you must be connected to the Internet.

Reports

The Report facility gives an overview of the Web site, providing statistics, name and sizes of files and the status of hyperlinks. The Site Summary is the main view, individual topics can be viewed in detail. Click the button to open the main report.

The specific items you need to check on the Report are Hyperlinks, Unverified and Broken hyperlinks.

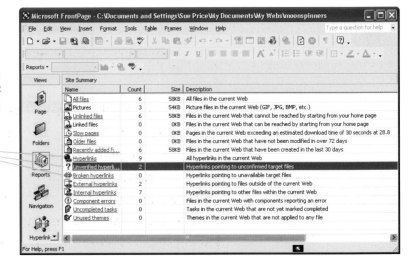

Unverified links occur if you mistype a URL, or if you change file names or locations after the page was created.

Always use the FrontPage Folder view if you need to change file locations as the links are automatically updated.

Click on Unverified hyperlinks in the Name column to see the itemised list of problems. You will be asked if you wish the links verified.

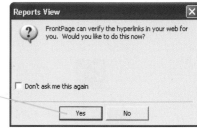

Click Yes to check the hyperlinks if you are connected to the Internet. To perform the check later, you can use the Verify Hyperlink button on the Reports toolbar.

FrontPage checks the links and creates a new report. The Status bar shows the updated summary. One link is verified; the broken link is created by a mistyped URL.

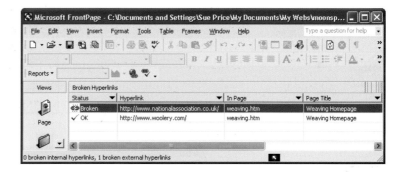

To amend the hyperlink, right click the incorrect URL and select Edit Hyperlink. You can Edit Page to return to the original location of the link. When you type the corrected name, FrontPage automatically checks again. The Report will be updated. Press F5 (Refresh), or select View, Refresh to update the details on the Status bar.

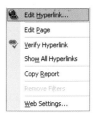

View in browser

See page 204 for checking links in Preview mode.

The page Preview mode lets you view your Web pages in a simulated browser view. You need to check the pages in full browser mode, using your default browser and other browsers that your visitors might employ, to ensure that everything works as expected.

You can use the Preview in Browser button on the toolbar but to access all the options, you need to select File, Preview in Browser.

You will need to save the pages before you can view them in the browser.

The dialog box lists available browsers. Select the Add button to include a browser on your PC that is not currently listed.

Use the different browsers and resolutions to see how the pages might appear to visitors with different facilities.

Click Preview and a copy of the selected browser is loaded, allowing use of the full browser functions, including the Back and Forward buttons.

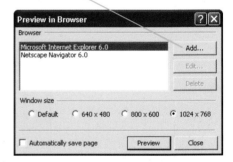

To return to FrontPage, click the Close button on the browser title bar.

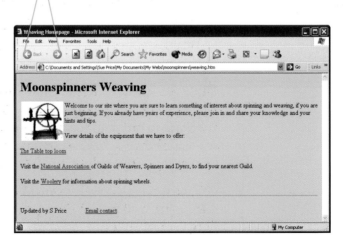

Hyperlinks view

The Hyperlinks view shows the links created, both internal and external. Select each page in turn to see the associated links. Any broken links are also identified. You can right click the hyperlink to repair it.

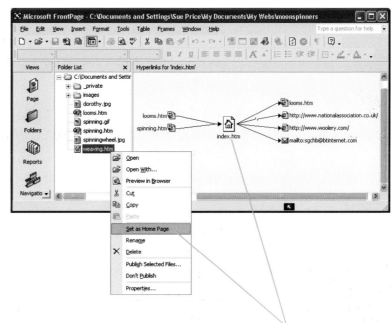

The name of the page in the Folder List may not change immediately.

For the CLAIT exercise specifying the Home Page in this way is not required.

2 Hyperlinks view can be used to define the home page for your Web site. Right click the main page, weaving.htm in the Folder List and select Set as Home Page. This changes its name to index.htm and updates all links to the page.

When you visit a Web site, you normally specify the name of the Web site without any page names. The browser will search through a list of standard names such as index.htm, default.htm, index.html and default.html. It will display the first match. If you name your Home page differently, your Web site may not be found.

URLs are case sensitive, so it is also important to use a consistent rule, to name all your Web pages and files. The best choice it to always use lower case.

Printing Web page and html

See page 79 for more information on printing from Internet Explorer.

For the CLAIT exercises, you must print a copy of the Web page as it would appear on the Internet, and of the underlying source code.

With your Web pages open, select Preview in Browser. All printouts will be the same, whatever the size of the browser window or the screen resolution.

You must print from the browser view to include the file information in the footer area.

Use Page Setup and Print Preview in the browser to make sure that there are no problems with the document.

The printed page will normally print without the background fill colour. It should include a header to indicate the particular page, such as Home Page. It should also include a footer with the file source information.

You will need to print each page in both views. There is no option to print all the Web pages at once.

The print of the HTML source code provides proof of the hyperlinks and the use of background colour.

Switch to the HTML view and select Print. When you are in the HTML view, be very careful not to make any inadvertent changes.

You can print the HTML code from the browser window. Select View, Source. It will open in a copy of NotePad, the plain text editor.

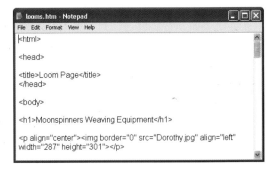

Publish your Web

New CLAIT will not require you to Publish your Web in any of the exercises.

Your ISP will provide access to the Internet, storage space for your Web files and other services. UK ISPs include BT Web World, Dial Pipex and Freeserve.

To make your Web available to visitors on the Internet, you must copy all the files and folders to the Web server managed by your Internet Service Provider (ISP). The method used to Publish your Web depends on whether your ISP offers a Web server with FrontPage Server Extensions services installed. The server extensions are not essential, but with them available you can take advantage of extra functions such as forms and counters, and use FrontPage to maintain your files and hyperlinks. Each time you publish the Web, FrontPage compares the files on your local computer to the files on the Web server. If you move a file in your Web on the hard disk, FrontPage will update and correct any hyperlinks to it, and then make the same corrections to the Web server files, the next time you publish the Web. FrontPage uses HTTP (Hypertext Transfer Protocol) to transfer the files.

If your ISP does not support the server extensions, your Web must be published using FTP (File Transfer Protocol) and you will have to manage the file and hyperlink changes yourself.

1 Open the Web and click the Publish button (or select File, Publish Web) to start the process.

The next time you press the Publish button, FrontPage will remember the address last used, and this step will be skipped. Use File, Publish Web to specify a different address.

2 Enter the Web site URL or the FTP address for the Web server providing your Web space.

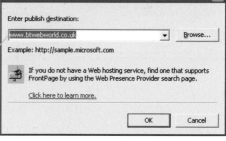

Your ISP will give you the addresses and the sign on details that you need to access the Web server and transmit your files.

3 Enter the required account ID or user name and password, and then click OK.

4 FrontPage connects to the Internet and transfers the files.

Exercise

You are allowed two hours to complete this exercise.

Scenario

You are working in the Promotion Department of 'Surprise Gardens'. Your job is to help develop the company Web pages. Your manager has two pages prepared, which need to be linked.

These are the files:

surprise.htm	the 'Surprise Gardens' homepage
centres.htm	a page listing the individual centres.

The Web pages are in the Unit 9 WEB folder section of the New CLAIT in easy steps data files downloaded from the In Easy Steps Web site (see page 233).

1. Create a link in the surprise.htm page as follows:
   Text to be linked: Garden Centre Locations
   Link to: centres.htm
   Enter your name and exam centre number after the text:
   Updated by .... Save the amended surprise.htm page.

2. Create a link in the centres.htm page as follows:
   Text to be linked: Surprise Gardens
   Link to: surprise.htm
   Enter your name and exam centre number after the text:
   Updated by.... Save the amended centres.htm page.

3. Reload each page in the browser and test the links.

You have been asked to make a new page with location information for one of the centres. The new page must be formatted according to the company's Web design policy as shown in the diagram.

4. Create a new page and insert the text file heronsbrook.txt.
   Enter your name and exam centre number after the text:
   Updated by:

5. Format the text Surprise Gardens as Heading 1 (large font).
   Format the text Heronsbrook Garden Centre as a
   Subheading (medium font size).
   Format all other text as Body Text (small font size).
   Ensure that each paragraph is separated by a clear linespace.

6. Format all the text to be centre-aligned on the page.
   Embolden the text MapQuest Web site.
   Italicise the text "Please make it soon".

The page must include the map for Heronsbrook Garden Centre.

The text and the graphic files will also be found in Unit 9 WEB folder section of the New CLAIT in easy steps data files.

7   Import the graphic heronsbrook.gif and position it below the text 'Heronsbrook Garden Centre', and above the text 'This map has been provided'.
Make sure that the graphic is centre-aligned on the page.
The new page should link back to the 'Surprise Gardens' homepage.

8.   Create a link in the new page as follows:
Text to be linked: Surprise Gardens
Link to: surprise.htm
Save the new page as heronsbrook.htm.

The 'Surprise' page should have a link to the new page.

9.   In the centres.htm page, locate the text Heronsbrook.
Link this text to your newly created page, heronsbrook.htm.
Save the amended centre.htm page.

Load all the pages into the browser and test the new links.

10.   Change the background colour of the surprise.htm page ensuring that it is different from the text colour.
Save the amended surprise.htm page to disk.

Some of the links on the 'Surprise' homepage have not been completed.

11.   Create an external link in the surprise.htm page as follows:
Text to be linked: MapQuest Web site
External link to: www.mapquest.co.uk
Save the amended surprise.htm page.

12.   Create an e-mail link in the surprise.htm page as follows:
Text to be linked: Your name and exam centre number
External link to: enquiries@surprisegardencentres.co.uk
Save the amended surprise.htm page.

13.   Load the surprise.htm page into the browser, print a copy.
Load the centres.htm page into the browser, print a copy.
Load your new page into the browser and print a copy.
Print a copy of the HTML code used for each of the 3 pages.

14.   Close each document and exit from the application correctly.

Checklist

When you have finished the exercise, use the following checklist. Have you:

- Created a Web site using two supplied pages
- Created a new page using imported text and images
- Created and tested internal and external links
- Formatted the pages using standard styles as specified
- Entered text, as specified, and saved the updated files
- Printed pages in browser and HTML view

Answers

Centres

Surprise Gardens Home Page

Location

HTML

Presentation graphics

In this unit we use PowerPoint to develop an understanding of graphical presentation concepts. It covers creating a master layout, importing an image and applying standard formatting to create a consistent and professional document.

Covers

Unit Ten

Presentation graphics

PowerPoint is the presentation graphics program included with Microsoft Office. With it you can design, create and organise presentations in many formats, from handouts and transparencies, to sophisticated and automated shows run on the computer.

From the Taskbar, click Start, All Programs, Microsoft PowerPoint.

The term Slide refers to each page in a PowerPoint presentation, whether it is printed on paper, as a transparency, or just viewed in a screen show.

The program opens with the default blank presentation. The first view shows the Title slide in landscape layout, ready to begin a new presentation. The two text boxes are used as placeholders.

The Task Pane is a very useful addition to the PowerPoint window. Click View, Task Pane if it does not appear automatically.

PowerPoint provides an area for you to add speaker notes for each slide. These will not be displayed.

On the right, the Task Pane lists possible actions. PowerPoint, in common with many other Office programs, provides design templates and a Wizard to help with layout, colour and content.

The pane to the left allows you to switch between Outline and Slides view and provides an overview as you build the presentation.

Slide layouts

PowerPoint provides standard slide layouts, or templates, that you can use to present your information.

1 Click the down arrow on the New Presentation Task pane, and select Slide Layout to view the available layout templates.

◆ ◆ New Presentation ▼

2 Hover the mouse over each slide to see its name and style. The first block of four slides are for text only. The Title slide is displayed when you open PowerPoint.

3 The Title Only and Title and Text slides provide the layouts needed for the CLAIT exercises.

4 Content Layouts show a number of configurations. They include layouts with placeholders for tables, charts, Clip Art and WordArt. Scroll down to see other examples including Organisation charts. There is also a blank layout.

5 When you insert a new slide, select it from this Task pane. Click the arrow on the selected slide layout and choose Insert New Slide.

6 Note the checked box to show these designs when inserting new slides.

The Slide Master

You can apply a background colour in any view. Select Format, Background, and choose a colour. Lighter colours are better for printing purposes.

To create a professional looking presentation, you should implement a house style using a standard layout and consistent formatting. PowerPoint provides the Slide Master to enable you to do this. You can insert an image or background on the Slide Master, position text boxes, format text styles and add standard text. That configuration will be applied to all the slides in the presentation.

To create a Slide Master:

1   Select View, Master, Slide Master.

The Slide Master View toolbar will appear automatically when you display the Slide Master.

2   The Slide Master provides placeholders for a title, text content, and standard autotext areas for date/time, footer, and slide number. The text boxes can be resized and moved if required.

The only text you type on this slide is text that you want to appear on every slide.

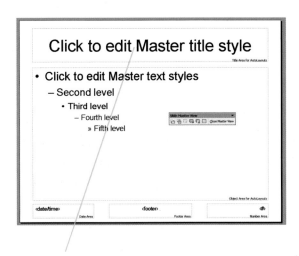

You may need to increase the size of the Title text box when applying large font sizes and attributes such as bold, see Unit 6, DTP, page 131 for resizing text boxes.

3   Click in the Title Area and use the Formatting toolbar to select the font size, style, alignment and attributes such as bold or italic that you wish to apply.

See page 221 for how to manage indentation and the hierarchical levels.

4 The main text box displays bulleted and indented text. Each level is represented by a different bullet style, size of font and degree of indentation. Select each level in turn and if necessary adjust the font size and any attributes.

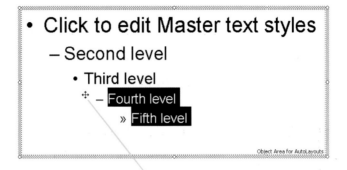

5 The Slide Master shows a hierarchy of five levels of bullets. The four-headed arrow that appears when the mouse is to the left of the text, allows you to select several levels and work with them as a group.

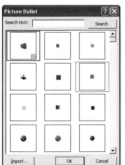

6 To change the bullet symbol, select Format, Bullets and Numbering and choose from the styles available. Click Customise to select a new style from a vast range of fonts. Click Picture to add even more stylish and coloured bullets. To remove Bullets, select None. You can apply and remove Bullets using the toolbar button which is a toggle switch.

The Numbering function works in the same way as the Bullets.

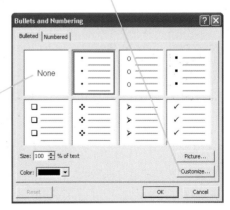

Slide Master text

The Slide Master is for design, colour, text and images that you want to show on every slide. Add the Title and other text in Normal view.

For text to appear on every slide in the same place, same font etc, you need to put it on the Slide Master. At the bottom of the Slide Master are three text areas.

The Date Area and the Number Area are autotext boxes. The data displayed in these frames is generated by PowerPoint.

1   You can delete the three frames in the footer area of the slide, and create a new text box for the required text. It will be displayed on all slides.

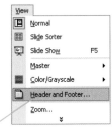

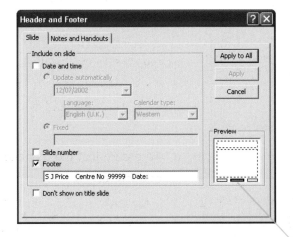

Selecting a Fixed date means you can type in the date to display.

2   Alternatively, select View, Header and Footer. This window lets you number the slides and use an automatic date.

You may wish to deselect the Date and time box, and add the date manually in the Footer box.

3   In the Preview pane, the Footer (central) box shows it is active. The Date and the Slide number boxes remain unchecked and are inactive. Type your text into the Footer and click on Apply to All.

Insert an image

1 With the Slide Master displayed, select Insert, Picture, From File. The default folder that opens is My Pictures. You may need to navigate the folders to locate the image.

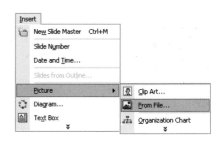

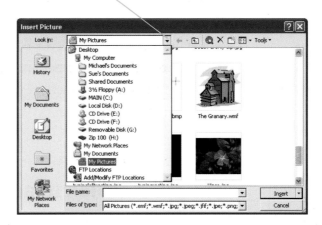

2 Click Insert and the selected graphic will be inserted centrally with its selection handles displayed. Drag it to the required position using the arrowhead mouse symbol.

3 To ensure that the text and image frames do not conflict, you may need to resize the text. Position the mouse on the selection handle and drag.

- **Click to edit Master text styles**
  - **Second level**
    - **Third level**
      - Fourth level
        - » Fifth level

Applying a slide layout

When you have created the Slide Master, save the file using the standard Office procedure and the supplied filename.

The completed Slide Master will provide the template for the slides you create in this presentation.

1 Select View, Normal to return to the standard slide view, or click on the Normal View icon at the bottom of the screen.

2 The text and image that were inserted onto the Slide Master are displayed and the standard Title slide layout applied.

For every Slide Master, you can create a Title Master. The Title Master adheres to the formatting applied to the Slide Master, but not the layout. You may need to amend the Title Master if there is a subtitle that causes a conflict between text and graphic.

You can select and delete any unwanted text boxes, such as the subtitle frame.

3 When the mouse is over a layout, the option box appears. Click the arrow to access the shortcut options. You can also just click the style you want to apply to it.

4 Add your text in the placeholders. When you click in the text area the existing text will disappear.

Bulleted text

The Slide Master showed the bullet levels and allowed you to specify the formats. See page 217.

PowerPoint provides five levels of bulleted text. Each bullet point is ascribed a level of importance, illustrated by the font size and degree of indentation. When the bullet point is promoted or demoted, both the bullet symbol and the text format are adjusted.

1   Select a layout that contains bulleted text. The bullets appear automatically on the first line and as you press Enter.

The Increase and Decrease Indent buttons can also be used to promote and demote bulleted text.

2   To apply a lower level bullet, or demote text, press Tab once for each level, before you begin to type. Use Shift+Tab to promote text.

3   You can drag a bullet to promote or demote. The text will move one level at a time. Any lower level points will also be adjusted.

For consistency on your slides, any changes to the bullet layout should be made on the Master slide.

- **Beginner's Guide**
- **Word Processing**
  - Spreadsheets

- **Beginner's Guide to**
  - Word Processing
    - Spreadsheets

4   Bullet spacing and indentation is controlled through the Ruler, available on the View menu.

View
- Normal
- Slide Sorter
- Slide Show   F5
- **Ruler**
- Header and Footer...
- Zoom...

5   Drag the top triangle marker to move the bullet point, or the lower triangle marker to move the text. To move both and keep the existing spacing relationship, drag the rectangle on the bottom marker. You cannot promote or demote bullets this way.

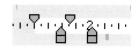

- **Beginner's Guide**
  - Word Processing
  - Spreadsheets

Text tools

For New CLAIT
purposes Autofit
Text may cause
problems as a
specific text size
is required.

Autofit Text

PowerPoint provides an Autofit Text
option that may adjust the text size to fit
the placeholder. A Smart Tag appears
when the amount of text will overfill the
frame. You will need to evaluate each
situation individually to see
the effect. In some instances
the line spacing is slightly
adjusted, in others the text is
resized. Click on control
AutoCorrect options to make
changes to the AutoFit setup.

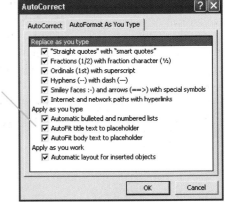

The Spell Checker

From the Menu
select Tools,
Options and the
Spelling and
Style tab.

Automatic spell checking
should be enabled when you
start PowerPoint. Any
misspelled words will be
underlined in red. Note that
the default option is to ignore words in
uppercase and words with numbers, so
proof reading is essential. Click the Style
Options button to see the underlying
concepts of standard design, such as upper
and lowercase conventions and number of
bullet points per slide.

Find and Replace

PowerPoint offers
a subset of the
Word Find and
Replace facility,
as slides generally
contain minimal text.

From the Menu select Edit, Find. Type in
the 'Find What' text and click the Replace
button to display the
Replace With box.
Replace works
forwards from the
cursor, Replace All
covers the whole
document and will
inform you of the
number replaced.

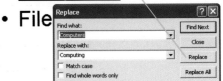

Arranging slides

The standard PowerPoint window displays an extra pane with Outline and Slides views. The Outline view shows the slide text, so you can see the development of your document. The Slides view gives the impression of layout, spacing and overall presentation. The Slides view also enables you to change the order of the slides. However, if you have lots of slides use Slide Sorter View.

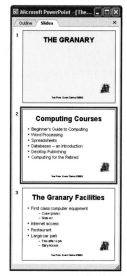

To change the magnification of either of these panes, click on the pane and use the standard zoom option.

Change the width of the pane using the double headed arrow that appears on the dividing bar.

1 Select View, Slide Sorter.

2 Click on the slide you wish to reposition and drag it to its new location. You will see the Move symbol attached to the mouse, and a large vertical line indicating its new position.

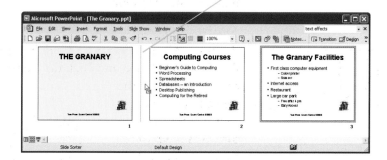

If you wish to start and end with the same slide, Slide Sorter view allows copy and paste of slides.

3 Slide Sorter view is used to set up an automated show. Transition effects, such as checkerboards and blinds, can be applied and the show previewed. See page 225 for more details on slide shows.

Printing slides and handouts

You will usually be expected to print the slides, one per page, and thumbnail or handouts at a specified number per page.

1 Select File, Page Setup. The slides are sized for an On-screen show, but you may wish to select a paper size.

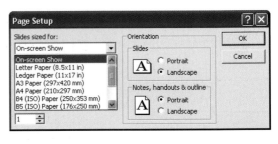

2 Select File, Print, to view all the printing options. Slides are the default choice, and will be printed one slide per page in landscape orientation.

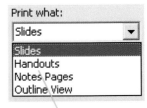

It's a good idea to proof read the finished prints. Errors are much more easily spotted on paper.

3 To print reduced size slides, or Thumbnails, select Handouts from the Print What box. Select the number per page, from one to nine. The slides will print lines for audience notes at the side if you select three per page.

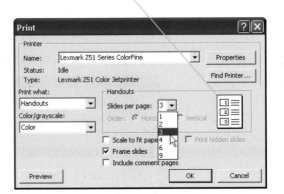

4 PowerPoint makes it easy to share presentations, offering Send to Mail Recipients (for Review) or (as Attachment). It also provides a Pack and Go Wizard to enable you to transfer the presentation to another computer.

The Slide Show

1 Select Slide Sorter view, and pick the Slide Transition Task pane.

2 Transition effects are applied as the slide appears on the monitor. Select a slide and choose a Transition effect.

3 Some effects can be quite dramatic, so it is best to stay with the same one or two throughout the show.

4 The speed can be adjusted, and sound applied. For fully automated shows, you can choose to advance to the next slide automatically after a set time.

5 Click the Slide Show button to go straight to the show. Click the mouse to proceed from slide to slide. The show will end with a black screen. Click the mouse, or press Escape to return to the PowerPoint editing view.

6 The slide text can be animated. Switch to Normal view and select the Slide Design – Animation Scheme Task pane. Click the Play button to see the effect.

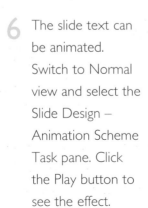

The Granary Facilities

- First class
  – colour printer
  – scanner
- Internet access
- Restaurant
- Large
  – Free
  – Easy

Sue Price Exam Centre 99999

Exercise

You are allowed two hours to complete this exercise.

Scenario

You are working as an assistant for Surprise Gardens. You have been asked to provide a slide show presentation for the headquarters foyer.

You have to produce a presentation of three slides.

1. Create a master slide as follows:
   Create a page-wide title frame at the top of the page.
   Create a page-wide main frame below the title frame.
   Set up the text styles in these frames as follows:

Frame	Style	Emphasis	Size	Bullets	Alignment
Title	Title	Bold	48	No	Centre
Main	1st level	None	32	Yes	Left
Main	2nd level	Italic	24	Yes	Left and Indented

You'll find the Surprise Logo image in the Unit 10 PRG folder, in the New CLAIT in easy steps data files downloaded from the In Easy Steps Web site (see page 233).

Place the Surprise Logo image at the bottom right corner of the slide. Make sure it does not overlap the text frames.

Create a frame at the bottom of the page, below the main frame. Enter your name, exam centre number and today's date in this frame.

Format the background to be light green.

2. Save the master slide using the filename Garden Show. This master slide is to be used for all three slides.

3. Create slide 1 and enter the title SURPRISE GARDEN CENTRES. Leave the main frame blank for this slide.

4. Create slide 2 and enter the title Surprise Centre Locations. Enter the following text in the main frame, using the styles shown:

Englemere	1st level
Harlequin	2nd level
Heronsbrook	1st level
Avon	2nd level

Silverbrook	1st level
Rookery	2nd level
The Elms	1st level

5. Create slide 3 and enter the title Surprise Centre Amenities. Enter the following text in the main frame with the styles shown:

Good Visitor Amenities	1st level
Plentiful car parking	2nd level
Children's playground	1st level
Knowledgeable staff	2nd level
Amenities for the Disabled	2nd level

6. Save the slide show keeping the file name Garden Show

7. Print out each of the 3 slides, one per page.

You have been asked to make a few changes to the presentation.

8. On slide 2, delete the line Rookery

9. Add the following line to slide 3, after Plentiful car parking, and before Children's playground

Restaurant	2nd level

10. On slide 3, demote Children's playground. On the same slide, promote Knowledgeable staff and Amenities for the Disabled.

11. Replace the word Amenities with the word Facilities wherever it appears in the presentation (three times in all).

12. Save the amended slide show as Garden Show 2

13. Print a set of audience notes with 3 thumbnail slides on one page.

14. Close the presentation and exit the software correctly.

Checklist

When you have finished the exercise, use the following checklist. Have you:

- Used a presentation graphics program
- Created a Master slide, and set up the format for title and text
- Inserted an image file in the correct position
- Entered the correct text on the Master slide
- Saved the Master slide using the specified file name
- Entered the presentation text, as specified
- Checked that the text has maintained the correct font size and has not overlapped the image
- Used a background colour if required
- Promoted and demoted bulleted text
- Printed the presentation in slide and thumbnail format
- Saved the file using the correct name and closed the application

Answers

Slide 1

Slide 2

Slide 3

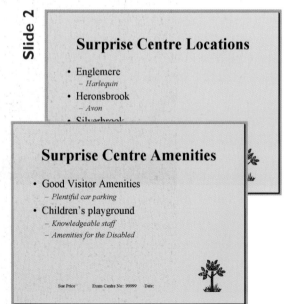

Handouts

Webwise, IC³ and Downloads

This section introduces the units that are supported by external tests - Webwise, and the three IC³ units. It provides some notes to help you select the appropriate units for your New CLAIT qualification. It also explains how to obtain the files that you need to make full use of the exercises in this book.

Covers

Units Eleven to Fourteen

Becoming Webwise

Becoming Webwise, the eleventh unit in the New CLAIT syllabus, is created and managed by the BBC, and accepted by OCR as an equivalent unit. You'll find the course on the BBC Web site at www.bbc.co.uk/webwise/learn/index.shtml.

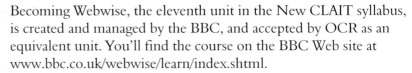

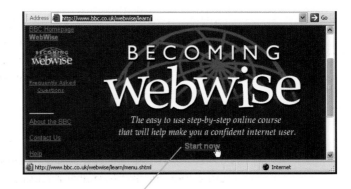

Click the link <u>Start Now</u> to try out the course without actually registering or enrolling at a centre.

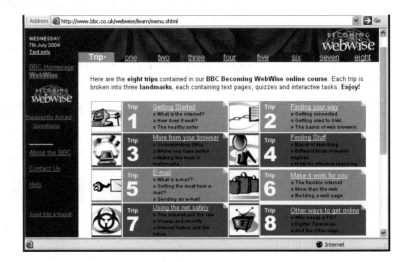

The course is made up of eight 'trips', each with various sections including quizzes and case studies. It covers the Internet, e-mail and some of the latest technology such as WAP phones. You should allow up to two hours for each 'trip'.

IC³ Certification

Internet and Computing Core Certification (IC³) is a validated, standards-based training and certification programme for basic computing and Internet knowledge and skills. There are 3 units, one or more of which may be included in your New CLAIT qualification, subject to the restricted combinations (see page 232).

IC³ Computing Fundamentals

This covers computer hardware, computer software and using an operating system, and the ability to identify different types of computers, the components of a personal computer and how these components work together.

The assessment for each IC³ unit takes the form of an on-line test using Certiport Software. It is composed of both practical tasks and multiple choice items. The whole test takes approximately 45 minutes to complete.

IC³ Key Applications

This unit includes standard functions in Windows applications, such as file management, editing and printing. It also covers functions specific to word processing and spreadsheets.

IC³ Living Online

This covers networks and the Internet, electronic mail, and using the Internet to browse and search for information, identifying different types of computer networks and communications networks.

For more information, including IC³ courseware and practice exams, visit the distributor's Web site at www.ic3cert.co.uk.

The IC³ units may be provided by awarding bodies other than OCR centres. However, the only way these units can contribute to achieving the NQF-accredited New CLAIT qualification is if they have been achieved through an OCR centre as part of the OCR CLAIT Suite.

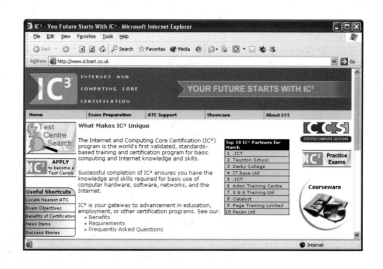

Choosing units

To gain the CLAIT certificate you must successfully complete five units. Using a Computer, Unit One, is mandatory. It covers the most basic functions, such as opening a file, entering text, saving and closing a file. It would make sense to take Unit Two, Word Processing, but it is not mandatory.

It may be that if you are taking the course at a registered centre, your choice is restricted. Some centres may only offer the more mainstream units – Using a Computer, Word Processing, Electronic Communication, Spreadsheets and Database. The extra units could be offered separately or undertaken independently.

With a full choice of units, you could select subjects that suit your aptitudes or ambitions. For example, if you wish to use your skills in an office environment then the best choice is Word Processing, Spreadsheets, Databases and Electronic Communication.

With the help of this book, you are able to explore all of the units, even if your centre has a restricted choice.

For working in the media or publicity, include more graphical applications such as Desktop Publishing, Presentation Graphics and Web Pages.

For working in a creative arena, choose Web Pages and Computer Art. Word Processing and Electronic Communications fit well into all scenarios.

Undertaking all ten units, for examination purposes or not, would give you a sound understanding of computing software, functions and potential. The units build on each other to some degree, and knowledge gained in one can usually be applied to another. More advanced topics in Word, become the means of creating slides in PowerPoint; using text and image frames in Desktop Publishing is taken further in Computer Art.

Restricted combinations

For your New CLAIT qualification, you can claim only one of Unit 3 (Electronic Communication), Unit 11 (Becoming Webwise) and Unit 14 (Living Online), due to the overlap of Internet related content. Also, if you are claiming Unit 13 (Key Applications), you cannot claim Unit 2 (Word Processing) or Unit 4 (Spreadsheets), due to the overlap of application related content.

Download files

A number of exercises require data files to get you started. On a New CLAIT course, these would be provided by your tutor. If you are using this book for self study, you can download a full set of files at www.ineasysteps.com/books/downloads/

The folders include the files needed for the exercises described at the end of each unit. See page 122 for an example. Please note that only files required for the exercises can be downloaded.

1 Select the link click here to download the self-extracting file NewCLAIT_files.exe and save it onto your disk drive.

2 Double click the downloaded file to create the set of folders (Unit 1 to Unit 10). By default these will be generated on the floppy drive, or you can specify your hard disk.

Electronic Communications

The exercise for Electronic Communications starts with receiving an email with an attachment. You can request such an email at the Web site newclait.prient.co.uk.

This Web page also offers a link to the In Easy Steps download page.

Visit http://newclait.prient.co.uk and enter your e-mail ID, to request the e-mail message needed in the Unit Three exercise.

Where next?

As a first step, you could undertake the New CLAIT units that you did not do for examination purposes. This would help to round out the basics principles and tools of computing and give you a good grounding on which to build.

CLAIT Plus

You can find help and instruction as well as practice exercises in CLAIT Plus in easy steps (ISBN 1840782528). The book covers all nine Assignment units and includes information on the Solutions and MOS units.

As New CLAIT is the OCR Level 1 Certificate for IT Users, the next obvious step for those who are successful is to take CLAIT Plus, the Level 2 Certificate for IT Users. This certificate follows the general approach set at Level 1.

In CLAIT Plus you will be required to take a mandatory core unit plus three optional units from a large selection of topics. The Core unit is Create, Manage and Integrate Files. The Optional units are the same as those offered at Level 1 for the most part. However, OCR have also introduced a new 'Solutions' based approach for Spreadsheets, Databases, Desktop Publishing and Presentation Graphics, as an alternative approach. This would enable a student to design his own assignment, from perhaps a workplace environment, as long as it matched and demonstrated compliance with the OCR assessment criteria. As in New CLAIT Level 1, you are advised to take units that suit your interests and needs or workplace requirements.

CLAIT Advanced

When you have achieved the certificate at CLAIT Level 2, you may be advised to explore the options open to you within the CLAIT Plus syllabus before progressing onto Level 3.

For more details on the CLAIT levels visit the OCR Web site at: www.ocr.org.uk/schemes/it/newclait/home.htm.

ECDL

The European Computer Driving Licence encompasses some of the CLAIT Level 1 and CLAIT Plus syllabi. It covers seven topics: Basic Concepts of IT, Using the Computer and Managing Files, Word Processing, Spreadsheets, Databases, Presentations, and Information and Communication. It presumes no previous computing knowledge, and aims to cover basic understanding and competence in using a computer.

For more information, visit the ECDL Web site at: www.ecdl.com.

Index